Endangered Species

Karin Vergoth &
Christopher Lampton

Endangered Species

revised
edition

An Impact Book

Franklin Watts
A Division of Grolier Publishing
New York • London • Toronto • Sydney
Danbury, Connecticut

Photographs ©: BBC Natural History Unit: 66 (Bengt Lundberg), 33 (John Sparks), 30; Corbis-Bettmann: 32 (Grant Smith), 41 (UPI), 36, 52; Jeff Vanuga: 38; Lynn M. Stone: cover right, 48; Photo Researchers: 63 (Peter B. Kaplan), 85 (Carl D. Koford/National Audubon Society), 53 (Tom McHugh), 69 (Tom McHugh/Steinhart Aquarium), 80 (Dan Suzio); Tom Stack & Associates: 13 (Thomas Kitchin), 12 (John Shaw); Tony Stone Images: 76 (Jim Nilsen); Visuals Unlimited: cover left (Walt Anderson), 90 (Marc Epstein), 51 (John Sohlden), 44.

Insert # 1 photographs ©: BBC Natural History Unit: 8 (Thomas D. Mangelsen); Photo Researchers: 9 (A. Rider), 5 (Scott Camazine/Sue Trainor); Tom Stack & Associates: 4 (John Gerlach), 2 (Mark Newman), 3 (Brian Parker), 7 (Greg Vaughn); Tony Stone Images: 1 (Johnny Johnson); Visuals Unlimited: 6 (Walt Anderson).

Insert # 2 photographs ©: BBC Natural History Unit: 2 (Pete Oxford), 10 (Lynn M. Stone); Jeff Vanuga: 4; Lynn M. Stone: 5; Photo Researchers: 7, 8 (Francois Gohier); Tom Stack & Associates: 11 (John Cancalori), 9 (Joe McDonald), 1 (John Shaw), 3 (Larry Tackett); Visuals Unlimited: 6.

Illustrations by George Stewart and Joe LeMonnier

Visit Franklin Watts on the Internet at:
http://publishing.grolier.com

Library of Congress Cataloging-in-Publication Data

Vergoth, Karin.
    Endangered species / Karin Vergoth and Christopher Lampton. — Rev. ed.
        p.   cm.—(An Impact book)
    Rev. ed. of Endangered species / Christopher Lampton, 1988.
    Includes bibliographical references and index.
    Summary: Explains what species are, how they become extinct, and the effect of extinction on the ecosystems, and surveys endangered species of plants and animals and possible solutions.
    ISBN 0-531-11480-5 (lib. bdg.)   0-531-16438-1 (pbk.)
    1. Endangered species—Juvenile literature. 2. Endangered plants—Juvenile literature. 3. Extinction (Biology)— Juvenile literature. 4. Wildlife conservation— Juvenile literature.   [1. Rare animals. 2. Rare plants. 3. Endangered species. 4. Extinction (Biology) 5. Wildlife conservation.]   I. Lampton, Christopher. II. Lampton, Christopher, Endangered species. III. Title.
QL83.V47   1999
578.68—dc21

98-8197
CIP
AC

Contents

Chapter 4
Can We Stop the Extinctions?

Endangered Species

The Next Great Dying

There are some things money can't buy. One of them is a live dinosaur. Try though you might, you'll never find a living dinosaur for sale. If you're lucky, you may find enough pieces of a dinosaur to put a skeleton together. If you have enough money, you may even be able to buy a dinosaur skeleton. Not long ago, the largest and most complete *Tyrannosaurus rex* skeleton ever found was bought at an auction by the Field Museum in Chicago for $7.6 million. But a fossilized skeleton, or a fossilized dinosaur egg, is as close as you'll ever get to owning the real thing.

Of course, everybody knows that you can't buy a live dinosaur, or even find one. Dinosaurs lived on Earth a long time ago, but now they're gone. Nothing can bring them back. Dinosaurs became extinct 65 million years ago. They were wiped out by a deadly catastrophe that many scientists believe was triggered by a huge comet or asteroid crashing into Earth.

It wasn't only the dinosaurs that became extinct in this "great dying"; scientists estimate that up to 90 percent of all other species living at that time disappeared as well. Because so many species died off in a fairly short period of time, we refer to this great dying as a *mass extinction*. Scientists who study the remains of ancient life tell us that there have been five major mass extinctions in our planet's long history. Each one was caused by natural events, such as the changes in Earth's climate that caused the ice ages or the impact of comets and asteroids.

We're in the middle of another mass extinction right now. Many people are calling it the "Sixth Extinction." But unlike past extinctions, this one isn't being caused by icy rocks from space or sudden changes in the climate. It is being caused by humans.

And it's happening much faster than the *natural rate of extinction*—the rate at which living things have disappeared over millions of years of Earth's history. It's difficult to say how much faster the present extinction is progressing because most of the species going extinct are unknown to science. Plus, scientists aren't really sure how many species there are on Earth. They've identified about 1 million different plants, animals, and other life forms, but that's just a drop in the bucket. Most scientists believe there are probably about 10 million species on Earth, and some think there may be as many as 100 million species.

So how many species are becoming extinct? Let's first consider the natural rate of extinction. If there were just 1 million species on Earth, and scientists could check up on each species every year to see if it was still surviving, they would expect that about one species would become extinct each year. Of course, scientists can't track all species that closely—but they do keep close tabs on birds. There are about 10,000 species of birds. If birds were going extinct at the natural rate, one bird should be lost to extinction about *every* 100 years. What scientists are actually seeing is that one or more birds are going extinct each year. This means that the actual rate of extinction today is 100 times greater than the natural rate of extinction. That's alarming!

Taking all species of animals and plants together, scientists estimate that during the past century, the actual rate of extinction has been 100 to 1,000 times greater than expected. If there are indeed 10 million species on the planet, then 30 species are going extinct each day. In the next century, scientists predict the actual rate of extinction may be as much as 10,000 times greater than the natural extinction rate. In fact, some scientists warn that by the middle of the next century—about 50 years from now—half of all the species now living on Earth may be extinct. Another great dying is in progress—and very little is being done to stop it.

How did this mass extinction come about? Scientists do not need to devise elaborate theories to explain this twentieth-century disaster. The causes are all around them. Human beings—through exploitation, neglect, and overuse of Earth's resources—are engaged in wholesale destruction of the other living organisms on this planet. We are killing off our fellow species at an appalling rate.

When a species becomes extinct, no power on Earth can bring it back. Nothing can bring back the dinosaurs. If a particular species of bird, plant, or insect ceases to exist, no amount of money can bring it back. Extinction is forever. It's far worse than the death of an individual organism. When an individual dies, the children of that individual survive to carry on the species. But when a species becomes extinct, there are no children. The last dinosaurs left behind no descendants—neither did the woolly mammoth, or the dodo bird, or the passenger pigeon. Each of these creatures is now absent from

The African cheetah has been displaced from its grasslands habitat.

Earth. If nothing is done, they will be followed into oblivion by the Bengal tiger, the California condor, and hundreds of other *endangered species*—species that are teetering on the brink of extinction at this very moment.

Dozens of species are nearing extinction right now. The African cheetah has been displaced from its natural home as humans convert its grasslands to pasture and farmland. The black rhinoceros is illegally hunted for its horns, which are used for medicines and dagger handles. The black-footed ferret was nearly starved out of existence when its food supply—prairie dogs—was eliminated by human hunting and disease. The cichlid, a small fish native to Lake Victoria in East Africa, was nearly wiped out when non-native Nile perch were introduced into the lake.

This Malawi cichlid can be found in Lake Victoria in Africa.

These are only a few of the species now on the road to extinction. And though you have probably heard about some of the most glamorous species in danger of extinction, many others are unknown to all of us. These unidentified plants, insects, and fungi represent a valuable part of life on Earth.

This book is about the mass extinction now in progress. In the pages that follow, you'll see how the *diversity* of living species on this planet came about, why this diversity is disappearing, why we should do everything in our power to stop this process, and why it is already too late to save many of the species that are about to vanish forever.

Chapter 1

Why Species Exist

Life on Earth comes in many forms. Look out the nearest window, and you'll see a few dozen—or even a few hundred—examples. We call these forms species. Human beings are one species of living organisms, as are dogs, cats, maple trees, and houseflies. In general, scientists classify two living organisms as different species if they look and behave differently. Obviously, a dandelion, a gerbil, an amoeba, and a Saint Bernard all belong to different species. Each of these creatures looks very different from the others.

Sometimes deciding whether two organisms belong to different species is a bit more difficult. Although a cocker spaniel and a German shepherd look different, they belong to the same species: *Canis familiaris,* the domestic dog. A shark and a dolphin both live in the ocean, are about the same size and color, and have similar fins, but they do not belong to the same species. How can this be? For two organisms to be considered members of the same species, they must be able to *interbreed*. In other words, a male and a female of the same species can produce offspring that, in turn, can produce offspring. A cocker spaniel and a German shepherd can produce *fertile* offspring—offspring that can reproduce—so they must belong to the same species. A shark and a dolphin, on the other hand, cannot produce offspring, and so must be classified as different species.

As you learned in the Introduction, most scientists think there are about 10 million different species of living organisms on Earth. Where did all these species come from? The answer lies in the distant past.

Ancient Origins

The origin of life on Earth is a subject of some debate among scientists, but we can sketch a rough picture of how early life may have developed.

The planet Earth was born about 4.5 billion years ago. At that time, it was a cooling ball of molten rock orbiting around the still-young Sun. As it cooled, low-lying plains filled with water and became oceans. Gases erupted from volcanoes, forming our planet's atmosphere. The early oceans and atmosphere were full of chemicals that would have killed human beings instantly. But these poisonous chemicals, combined with the energy from lightning bolts or volcanoes, provided a perfect environment for the construction of brand new *molecules*.

A molecule is a group of *atoms*—the tiny building blocks of all solids, liquids, and gases in the universe. Some of the molecules in the primitive seas were very large, consisting of dozens, hundreds, or even thousands of atoms. When lightning bolts or unfiltered rays of sunlight struck the water, or when the water was heated by lava from a volcano, these molecules fell apart and then recombined to form different molecules.

New molecules were formed at random, but within the laws of chemistry. After hundreds of millions of years, these random chemical reactions created a molecule that possessed an incredible property—it could make copies of itself.

How can a molecule make copies of itself? Looking back across more than 4 billion years, it's difficult to say, but we can make a good guess. It is likely that these primitive, self-replicating molecules used a technique similar to the one used by a modern self-replicating molecule called *DNA*. As you can see by looking at the illustration on the next page, DNA (deoxyribonucleic acid) molecules exist in long, threadlike structures called *chromosomes*. They are located in the nucleus of *every cell* in your body. All other living things—from aardvarks to cactuses to Japanese beetles—have DNA, too.

Each person has forty-six different kinds of chromosomes, but there are trillions of copies of these chromosomes inside the human body. When a cell splits in two to make new cells, the chromosomes copy themselves so each new cell can have its own set of chromosomes. The new chromosomes are assembled from extra molecules floating around in the *cytoplasm*, or liquid interior, of the cell.

The self-replicating molecules in the primitive seas had plenty of loose molecules—spare parts, if you will—from which to make copies of themselves. It didn't take long for the early oceans to fill up with these molecules, so eventually, the molecules had to compete for spare parts. The molecules that gathered spare parts most efficiently could copy themselves more quickly. These faster-producing molecules soon outnumbered their slower cousins. In addition, some of these early molecules may have preyed on other self-replicating molecules, dismantling them for construction materials. These predatory molecules would have become more abundant, too.

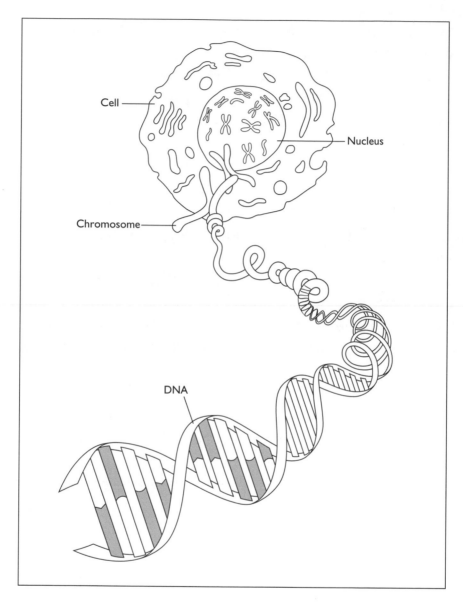

Cell

Nucleus

Chromosome

DNA

DNA (deoxyribonucleic acid) molecules exist in long, threadlike structures called chromosomes that are located in the nucleus of every cell. DNA contains the genetic or hereditary information for most organisms.

But wait a minute! If all these molecules were identical copies of the original self-replicating molecule, how could some have been better at making copies of themselves? The answer is that they were *not* identical. Occasionally, a molecule would make a mistake as it replicated itself and produce a flawed copy. Most of these flawed copies were worthless, incapable even of reproducing themselves. But occasionally one of these flawed copies was actually an improvement on the original. It was better than other molecules at collecting spare parts and reproducing itself.

Thus, over billions of years, the self-replicating molecules steadily improved themselves. As they made random mistakes—called *mutations*—copying themselves, some became better adapted to the world around them. They changed to meet the *environmental pressures* of their surroundings.

In time, some self-replicating molecules began to join together and form cells. And eventually some cells teamed up to form multi-celled organisms. Human beings are multi-celled organisms, as are all other living things large enough to see with the naked eye.

According to the theory of *natural selection*, an organism with traits well suited to its environment will survive and reproduce at a greater rate than organisms less suited to that environment. *Evolution* is the process of undergoing mutations that cause traits to change in ways that allow an organism to better face environmental pressures.

Working Together

As the self-replicating organisms developed more and more sophisticated ways of surviving in their environments, they also branched out to form many different kinds—that is, species—of organisms. This process is called *speciation*. It has occurred many times since living molecules first formed in the primitive oceans. For evidence, just look around at all the vast array of plants, animals, fungi, and microorganisms that now inhabit Earth. Amazingly, the species alive today represent only a fraction of those that have existed over the last 4 billion years.

Just as the self-replicating molecules competed with one another for the spare parts they needed to copy themselves, modern living organisms sometimes compete with one another for the food, shelter, and energy they need to survive. When one species loses this battle, it must either find a different environment or become extinct.

Sometimes, organisms cooperate. They adapt in ways that allow them to get the resources they need in different ways. When this happens, the species do not compete, and they can live together for long periods of time. If you study a natural environment, you'll see many examples of cooperation. One example of cooperation is the *food chain*.

To survive, all living things need energy. Energy is the force that allows organisms, and the molecules they are made of, to move. Even plants, which sometimes seem to be completely stationary, are full of movement on the molecular level. The first self-replicating molecules got their energy from the bolts of lightning, volcanoes, and storms that jostled Earth's early oceans. Today, the ultimate source of energy for most living things is the Sun. Unfortunately, we can't simply walk outside on a sunny day and absorb solar energy in a usable form. Only a few types of organisms—some kinds of bacteria, algae, and green plants—can use the Sun's energy directly.

When sunlight strikes the surface of a green plant, the plant "traps" the Sun's energy through a process called *photosynthesis*. This energy is then stored in molecules called *carbohydrates*, so the plant can use it later to power the activity of its cells.

An animal that eats the plant transfers the carbohydrates to its own body and can use the energy to power its own cells. For example, you can use the carbohydrates in foods such as bread, rice, and pasta to power your cells. An animal that eats the plant-eating animal will also receive the energy from the carbohydrates. Thus, the Sun's energy is passed from plants to *herbivorous* (plant-eating) animals to *carnivorous* (meat-eating) animals. This is an example of a food chain.

If it weren't for plants, most animals could not live. Plants—and other *photosynthesizers*—perform the important service of capturing the Sun's energy and putting it into a form that can be used by organisms that can't carry out photosynthesis.

Is this really cooperation? Are the plants building carbohydrates as a favor for animals—or are the animals stealing the carbohydrates from the plants? Do the plants want to be eaten?

In some cases, the answer is no. In fact, some plants have evolved elaborate defenses—thorns, poisons, or foul-tasting leaves—to prevent animals from eating them. (Of course, animals have in turn evolved ways of eating these plants anyway!) But in other cases, the plants produce fruits that are intended as food for animals. The fruits contain seeds. When an animal eats the fruit, it inadvertently spreads the seeds—either through messy eating or when the animal passes waste matter. The animal deposits the seeds in new locations, so young plants will not compete with their parents.

This exchange of services benefits everyone. Animals receive carbohydrate energy and molecular spare parts; plants have their offspring spread to remote corners of the landscape. By cooperating, both parties come out ahead in the evolutionary sweepstakes.

The interrelationships among living species are so complex that a given environment—a meadow, a swamp, or even a desert—is like a finely tuned machine in which every organism plays a part. If even a single organism is removed, the environmental machine will suffer. If enough organisms are removed, the machine will fall apart. In a sense, an environment is like a superorganism, and the individual organisms within the environment are the "cells" and "molecules" that make it up.

The study of environments and the individual organisms in them is called *ecology*. The environments themselves, along with the organisms that live in them, are called *ecosystems*.

How do ecosystems come into existence? They are the result of millions of years of natural selection. The result is a mixture of living things that can live together in a stable environment. During that time, individual organisms evolved in ways that helped them adapt to the environment. Natural selection tends to favor organisms that find cooperative rather than competitive ways of fitting into their environment. Thus, each organism must find its *ecological niche*—a way to survive in an ecosystem without conflicting with the ways other organisms survive in that ecosystem. Suppose two different grazing animals living together on the African plains both eat grasses. If they evolve to eat different kinds of grasses, they can live peacefully together. The kind of food an organism eats, the kind of shelter it requires, and the way it rears its young, all constitute its ecological niche.

Spreading the Genes

Although all living organisms are descendants of the self-replicating molecules found in Earth's primitive seas, most modern creatures are much more complex. Nevertheless, the chromosomes in our cells still closely resemble those original molecules.

Our chromosomes contain information written in a language called the *genetic code*. In effect, a set of chromosomes is like a cookbook. A cookbook contains directions for preparing all the dishes that make up a complete meal. Chromosomes contain instructions for building all the *proteins* that control how your body grows and functions. A cookbook is made up of many recipes, and a set of chromosomes is made up of many *genes*. Each recipe tells you how to prepare a specific dish, while each gene tells the body how to make a particular protein.

Like the first self-replicating molecules, when a modern organism reproduces—that is, has children—it passes on copies of its chromosomes, so that its offspring will be able to build the molecules they need to survive. However, if the organism practices sexual reproduction—and most familiar organisms do—then each offspring will receive half of its genes from each parent. Each organism has two genes for each characteristics, one from each parent. In the case of humans, if one parent has brown eyes and the other has blue eyes, their child may have either blue eyes or brown eyes, depending on which eye-color genes that child inherits.

You may be wondering what determines whether a child inherits a particular trait from its mother or its father. In other words, how does an organism know which gene recipe to use? Well, if both of the genes are identical—that is, if they contain recipes for the same protein—then there is no conflict. It doesn't matter which one is used. But if they are different, then the machinery inside the cell must decide which recipe to follow. As it turns out, some genes are used (or *expressed*) more frequently than others. *Dominant genes* are expressed more often than *recessive genes*. When the cellular machinery must choose between two different genes—one dominant and one recessive—it always chooses the dominant gene.

For instance, a human being with one gene for blue eyes and one gene for brown eyes will have brown eyes, because brown eyes are dominant over blue eyes. Recessive genes express themselves only when an individual receives them from both parents. Here's where things get a little confusing. If both parents carry a recessive gene for a certain characteristic, such as eye color, their child can ex-

Inheritance of Eye Color

Bb
(brown eyes) × **Bb**
(brown eyes)

	B	**b**
B	**BB** brown eyes	**Bb** brown eyes
b	**Bb** brown eyes	**bb** blue eyes

If both parents carry a recessive gene for eye color (b represents the gene for blue eyes), there is a 25 percent chance that their child will inherit the recessive gene from both of them and have blue eyes (bb).

press a trait different from the one expressed by either parent. For example, it is possible for both parents of a blue-eyed child to have brown eyes. If both parents have a recessive gene for blue eyes, there is a 25 percent chance that their child will inherit the recessive gene from both of them.

Why is it an advantage for genes to be shuffled around in this manner? If every member of a species had exactly the same genes, the species could live in only one kind of environment—the one that their genes were adapted for. If that environment changed, the identical individuals might all die. But if a species carries many different kinds of genes, and different members of that species receive different combinations of those genes, then that species will be able to live in several different environments. If one environment is destroyed, some members will be able to adapt to other environments. The total set of genes carried by all members of a species is called a *gene pool*. The more diversity in the gene pool—that is, the more varieties of genes that are available—the more likely that a species will be able to adapt to environmental changes.

New genes enter a gene pool through mutation—that is, through an accident that occurs when a chromosome makes a copy of itself. Some of these new mutated genes are improvements on the original. They increase the organism's chances of surviving and producing offspring. As a result, these new genes quickly spread through the population. But most mutated genes are not advantageous. If these bad genes are dominant, they will disappear rapidly from the gene pool. The individuals who inherit them will die before they can produce offspring. If the bad genes are recessive, many of the individuals who receive them will not express them. As a result, the bad genes may spread through the population. The bad characteristic will be expressed only when two organisms with the same bad gene produce offspring. This is how life-threatening genetic diseases such as hemophilia and cystic fibrosis spread through the human population.*

Fortunately, if the population size of a species is large, the odds of two individuals with the same bad gene coming together and producing offspring are small. Thus, large and medium-sized populations are generally healthier than small populations. In fact, if the population of a species grows very small, it will begin to suffer from *inbreeding depression*—many recessive genes expressing themselves in the same individual. Unless the size of such a population can be quickly increased, inbreeding depression can lead to species extinction.

What other factors can lead to extinction? That topic will be discussed in the next chapter. Now that you know why species exist and how they live together, let's look at the other side of the coin—how species cease to exist.

---

* For this reason, there are laws preventing closely related individuals, such as siblings and first cousins, from marrying. The chances are too great that they might be carrying the same recessive genes.

2

How Species Become Extinct

As you learned earlier, long before humans appeared on Earth, plant and animal extinctions—such as the mass extinctions that brought about the demise of the dinosaurs—were caused by natural events, such as cosmic disasters or changes in the climate. Although natural disasters still occasionally cause extinctions, most extinctions in the last few centuries have been the result of human activities. Even today, whether deliberately or inadvertently, humans continue to threaten the survival of countless species.

How do we threaten other species? Many species are threatened because we have destroyed their habitats. Others are threatened or have already been driven to extinction by overhunting.

Destruction of Habitat

Two thousand years ago, there were 250 million people living on Earth. It wasn't until about 1650 that the world population doubled to 500 million. By 1830, it had doubled again, reaching 1 billion.

The world population hit 2 billion by 1930, and 4 billion by 1974. Today, there are more than 6 billion people on Earth.

As the human population grows, more and more of the places where animals and plants live are destroyed or modified. Prairies and forests are converted to farmlands. Forests shrink as trees are cut for timber and paper. New roads cut through wilderness areas, opening up land previously unavailable for human use. Grasslands, forests, wetlands, and coastal areas are destroyed as cities and towns expand to accommodate more inhabitants.

In the last chapter, you learned that species evolve over long periods of time to fit into their ecosystems. The particular kind of ecosystem a species has adapted to is called its habitat. Some species—human beings are an especially good example—can survive in a wide variety of habitats, but many species cannot. Some creatures can survive only in wetlands or in fresh water or in forests. When one of these species loses its habitat, it must adapt to a new environment, move to a place similar to the lost habitat, or die.

Under natural conditions, environments change very slowly, so individual species have time to adapt to the changes. Humans, however, tend to change environments at a much quicker pace than nature does. As a result, the species that inhabit those environments have very little time to adjust. So, as certain habitats are destroyed to make room for human development, the species that need those habitats for their survival are being brought closer and closer to extinction.

This problem is most evident in the tropical areas of the world. Why? Because at least 50 percent of the species on Earth are found in tropical rain forests—and because these rain forests are currently being destroyed at an alarming rate.

Tropical rain forests are amazing environments. They cover roughly 3.5 million square miles (9.1 million sq. km) of land along the equator. Trees in a rain forest can tower more than 100 feet (30 m). Below these giant trees grow several levels of smaller trees. Within a rain forest are dozens—even hundreds—of different micro-climates, mini-ecosystems that contain unique collections of plant and animal species.

As you read this book, the world's rain forests are vanishing. By some estimates, nearly half of the rain forests that existed in 1950 have already been cut down. Today, they are being destroyed at a rate of about 40,500 square miles (105,000 sq. km) per year. That's an area the size of Kentucky. At this rate, there may be no rain forests left by 2050. And for every square mile of rain forest that is cut down, untold thousands of plants are killed, and an important animal habitat is lost.

Among large land animals, cats are most threatened by the destruction of the rain forests. Of the approximately twenty-five different cat species that live in tropical rain forests, fifteen are in danger of extinction. Plants are in jeopardy, too. There are literally millions of plant varieties in the world's tropical rain forests. Most of them have never been identified or cataloged by botanists. These plants exist only in the rain forest, and will cease to exist when the rain forests cease to exist. Since no one has yet cataloged all of the plant species that exist in the rain forests, it is difficult to say how often a species of rain forest plant becomes extinct, but some studies estimate that two to five plant species may be lost every hour.

Why are the rain forests being destroyed? Mostly, to make way for farming. In North America, the soil left behind when a forest is cleared is rich in nutrients and provides fertile land for farming. But

Large parts of the rain forest are being destroyed to clear land for farming. As a result, millions of plant and animal species are in danger.

most of the nutrients in a rain forest are contained within the plants themselves, not the soil. When the trees and other plants are chopped down, they leave behind nutrient-poor soil. This soil is not very good for farming. If the plants in the rain forest are burned after they are cut, some of the nutrients in the plants return to the soil as ashes. (This technique is known, for good reason, as *slash-and-burn agriculture*.)

Even so, the farmlands created in areas once covered by rain forests are good for no more than 2 or 3 years of farming. By then, all the nutrients are gone, and more rain forest must be destroyed to create new farmland. And so rain-forest destruction is an ongoing process that will continue as long as farmers try to grow crops there. In Brazil, the government is hoping to reduce slash-and-burn land clearing in the Amazon rain forest by offering incentives to farmers who plant crops or raise animals better suited to the existing ecosystem, such as fish farming.

Another type of environment that is being rapidly destroyed is wetlands—boundary areas where water and land ecosystems meet. Bogs, swamps, and marshes are all types of wetlands. Wetlands serve as the breeding grounds for many fish, birds, and other animals.

Because the soil beneath wetlands is rich with nutrients, many have been drained to create farms. Others have been filled in to create land for further development. At the turn of the century, the United States had more than 120 million acres (48 million ha) of wetlands—an area about twice the size of Oregon. By the mid-1980s, that number had been reduced to 80 million acres (32 million ha), about the size of Georgia and Florida. Wetlands are still disappearing today. Some states have lost more wetland areas than others. California has lost an estimated 90 percent of its wetlands.

As wetlands vanish, the species that live there vanish too. In the United States, wetlands are home to about 500 species of animals and 6,000 species of plants. Nearly 50 percent of the threatened and endangered animals in the United States, and more than 25 percent of the plants, depend on wetland habitats for their survival.

Changes in the Environment

It's not necessary to completely destroy a habitat to disrupt the lives of the species that live there. Sometimes relatively small changes to an environment are enough to wreak havoc with species that have spent millions of years evolving to fit that environment. This is illustrated most vividly in places where species have developed in a completely isolated environment, such as an island.

Islands play an important role in speciation (which, you'll recall, is the creation of new species). When members of a species become completely, or almost completely, isolated from others of their kind, they can evolve in different directions. If this separation continues for a long period of time, the organisms may evolve into a brand-new species that is incapable of breeding with its relatives in other parts of the world.

Charles Darwin, the naturalist who introduced the concept of natural selection in the nineteenth century, noticed this phenomenon while visiting the Galápagos Islands, which are off the coast of Ecuador. Different islands, he observed,

Charles Darwin

The black rhinoceros is illegally hunted for its horns, which are used to make medicines and dagger handles.

▲ The ring-tailed lemur of Madagascar is one of the most ancient primates surviving in modern times.

▼ The red panda lemur is one of nearly forty species of lemurs still surviving on Madagascar. At least ten species have become extinct in recent centuries.

The black-footed ferret, declared extinct in 1987, has bred well in captivity. In the early and mid-1990s, small populations were introduced into Wyoming and South Dakota.

This Bengal tiger is one of the roughly 6,000 tigers surviving in the wild today. They are in danger of extinction because their forest habitat is being destroyed throughout Asia and because tiger parts are used to make medicines.

The passenger pigeon, once the most common bird in North America, was hunted to extinction in the nineteenth century. The last passenger pigeon died in captivity in the Cincinnati Zoo in 1914.

▲ The right whale got its name because it was the "right" whale to hunt—easy to kill and rich with oil and bone.

▼ Over the centuries, whalers have also hunted sperm whales, like the one shown here, and bowhead whales, pushing each to the verge of extinction. The nations that form the International Whaling Commission voted to ban commercial whaling in 1982.

▲ In the Middle East, the oryx has been hunted for centuries, and today exists only in protected reserves.

▼ Grizzly bears have been hunted because they are considered a threat or a nuisance.

Only about 200 takahes exist today in New Zealand. Deer brought to the takahe's native Pacific Islands competed with the birds for the available food.

Many of the species that live on the Galápagos Islands are found nowhere else in the world.

had their own unique species of finch—a small bird. Darwin theorized that several groups of finches had migrated from the mainland thousands of years earlier. Each group had subsequently evolved separately until several new finch species had developed.

Since new species evolve more readily on islands than elsewhere, you might guess that a large percentage of the species on this planet are found on islands. And you would be right. The spectacular island of Madagascar, located off the coast of Africa, is home to as many as 150,000 species of plants and animals that exist nowhere else in the world. Even the story of Madagascar's birth is spectacular.

The continents and islands on Earth's surface, or crust, are in constant motion. Their movement is powered by hot rock in Earth's semi-liquid *mantle*—the layer between the crust and the core. About 250 million years ago, all the continents on Earth formed one mighty supercontinent called Pangaea. Around 180 million years ago, that supercontinent broke up. By 65 million years ago, the continents we know today had formed.

Long ago, Madagascar was part of the land mass that we now call Africa. Then, more than 100 million years ago, Madagascar split off from mainland Africa and drifted eastward. It is now 250 miles (400 km) east of Africa in the Indian Ocean.

When Madagascar was last in contact with Africa, mammals—now the dominant type of large animal on Earth—had just begun to develop, and the primate ancestors of human beings had not yet appeared. Evolution on Madagascar took its own course. Not surprisingly, human beings never evolved there, but the lemur—the most ancient of primates surviving into modern times—thrived.

Giant birds also evolved in Madagascar's vast forests. One of these—the *Aepyornis*, or elephant bird—was probably the heaviest

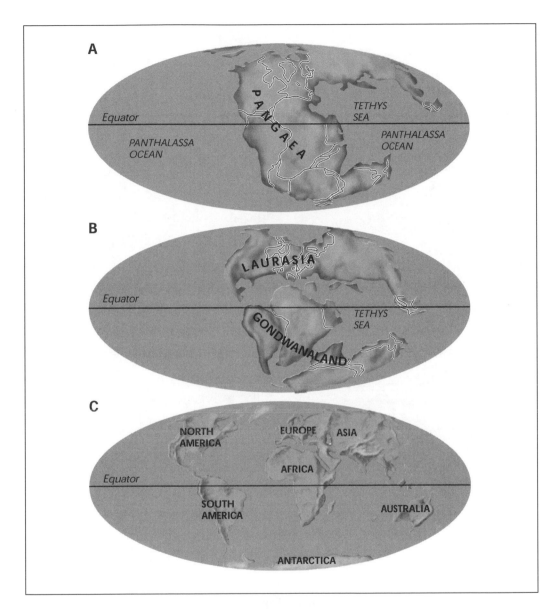

Millions of years ago all the land on Earth formed a single supercontinent called Pangaea (A). As time passed, Pangaea broke into two large continents called Laurasia and Gondwanaland (B). The continents we know today formed about 65 million years ago (C).

The tallest bird in Earth's history was the now-extinct giant moa from New Zealand. This flightless bird reached a height of 13 feet (4 m).

bird that ever lived on Earth. The *Aepyornis* was too large to fly. It weighed as much as 1,000 pounds (453 kg) and stood up to 10 feet (3 m) tall. (The tallest bird in Earth's history was the now extinct *Dinornis*, or giant moa, of New Zealand. It reached a height of 13 feet [4 m]).

Because evolution on Madagascar proceeded in isolation for so long, the island produced a host of species *indigenous* to the island. These creatures evolved there and nowhere else. Nearly forty indigenous species of lemurs still survive on Madagascar. In addition, 95 percent of all reptiles, 99 percent of all frogs, 80 percent of all flowering plants, and 42 percent of all birds found on the island live nowhere else in the world. And, because the landscape of Madagascar features a number of different environments—desert, rain forest, and dry forest—there are many different species of these plants and animals.

Many centuries ago, human beings arrived on Madagascar and began to disrupt this ecosystem. In this century, advances in medical technology have allowed the human population of Madagascar, the Malagasy people, to greatly increase. As a result, human beings have begun to threaten the impressive evolutionary experiments that nature has performed on Madagascar.

When humans arrived on Madagascar, 80 percent of the island—an area about the size of New Mexico—was covered with forest. Now forests cover less than 20 percent of the island. Most of this forest has been burned for farmland. The Malagasy people are subsistence farmers, clearing land to grow rice. While it's hard to argue with the need for farms, this wholesale loss of habitat has resulted in a high rate of extinction on Madagascar. At least ten species of lemur have become extinct in recent centuries. Of the nearly forty that remain, more than half are in danger of extinction.

On Madagascar, the loss of the forests is exacerbated by a high degree of *erosion*. As a result, existing farmland is being destroyed at a rate of 2 million acres (809,400 ha) a year. That's an area of land about the size of Yellowstone National Park! According to a report published by the World Bank, Madagascar's erosion problem is the worst on Earth. To replace the farmland destroyed by erosion, still more forests must be destroyed.

Government officials estimate that the forest—and the plants and animals that live there—are disappearing at a rate of 375,000 acres (151,760 ha) each year. That's an area of land as large as Chicago and New York City combined. One ecological expert calls the Madagascar problem "the single highest conservation priority in the world." Emergency efforts are being made to save the unique species of Madagascar from what seems to be their inevitable fate. The Malagasy government recently announced a plan to set aside

840 square miles (2,175 sq. km) of hardwood forest as a park. Some of the rarest animals in the world now live in Masoala National Park, including the red-ruffed lemur, the Madagascar red owl, and the serpent eagle.

It is not necessary that a species live on an island to have its life fatally disrupted by a single change in the environment. Consider the case of the black-footed ferret.

The black-footed ferret is one of the rarest mammals in North America. It attained that distinction because it has an extremely narrow, inflexible ecological niche. The black-footed ferret eats only prairie dogs. It even lives in abandoned prairie dog dens.

The endangered black-footed ferret was nearly starved out of existence when human hunting and disease eliminated prairie dogs, the ferret's major source of food.

In the 1930s, an extensive campaign was waged to exterminate the prairie dog, which farmers considered a destructive pest. The black-footed ferret, already rare, became rarer still as its source of food vanished. (Eating the poisoned carcasses of prairie dogs didn't help the ferret population either.) By the 1960s, the black-footed ferret was believed to be extinct. Then, in September 1981, a colony of the ferrets was discovered in Meeteetse, Wyoming, where prairie dog communities still thrived. The colony was small—just over 100 animals. In 1984, the colony was struck by disease, and about half of the ferrets died. In 1987, the few remaining black-footed ferrets were brought into captivity. The black-footed ferret was officially extinct in the wild.

The story of the black-footed ferret has a happy ending, at least for the present. The U.S. Fish and Wildlife Service teamed up with other state and federal agencies to carry out the Black-footed Ferret Recovery Program. The ferrets captured in 1987 bred well in captivity, and in the early and mid-1990s, small populations were reintroduced into the wild in Wyoming, Montana, and South Dakota. Those populations have grown, but the total number of ferrets is still quite small (less than 600), so the animals remain susceptible to outbreaks of disease.

Overhunting

About 10,000 years ago, most humans stopped relying on hunting to survive. They settled down in communities and began to grow crops and domesticate farm animals. But humans didn't stop hunting altogether. They continued to hunt for food, for sport, and for animal by-products, such as furs and oils. Many humans still hunt today.

The rhinoceros is hunted for its horn, which is used to make dagger handles or ground up and used in medicines. Some scientists have estimated that 90 percent of all adult rhino deaths are the result of *poaching* to obtain the horn.

The tiger faces a similar fate. At the beginning of this century, about 100,000 tigers lived in the wild. Today, as few as 6,000 still survive. The decline in wild tigers is due in part to the loss of their forest habitat throughout Asia, but tigers are also the victims of poaching. Tiger bone is used as an ingredient in traditional Asian medicines, as are other tiger parts. And despite laws that prohibit the hunting and sale of tiger products, these practices continue, and the tiger remains an endangered species.

Because humans are skilled, proficient hunters, any animal that people target is in danger of extinction. The most spectacular example of an animal hunted to extinction—in modern times, anyway—occurred in this century. The victim was the passenger pigeon, once the most common bird in North America, and possibly the most common bird on Earth.

The passenger pigeon was a large bird that lived in the forests of North America. When the first settlers arrived on the continent, they found what French explorer Samuel de Champlain called "an infinite number of pigeons," an estimate that wasn't as far-fetched as it sounds. The total population of passenger pigeons was certainly in the billions. As flocks of more than 100 million birds migrated northward and southward across the continent, the flapping of their wings was "like the roar of distant thunder," according to the famous naturalist John James Audubon. When flocks of these birds flew overhead, they blocked out the Sun. Passenger pigeons could do considerable damage to a forest just by settling onto the branches of its

A painting of passenger pigeons

trees. It wouldn't take long for the ground below their roosting spot to be buried under several feet of droppings.

The passenger pigeon was a successful species. It was well adapted to its environment. But in a world dominated by human beings, it had made a crucial evolutionary mistake—it was delicious to eat. Purveyors of gourmet food were willing to pay cash on the spot for dead passenger pigeons, and greedy hunters were more than willing to supply the carcasses. As passenger pigeons migrated, parties of hunters waited for them at their nesting grounds and slaughtered them as they landed in the trees.

But even wholesale slaughter seemed insufficient to exterminate a species as common as the passenger pigeon. How could mere human beings armed with guns threaten the future of a species that numbered in the billions? Quite easily, as it turned out. On March 24, 1900, a young hunter in Ohio shot the last passenger pigeon ever seen in the wild. A few years later, on September 1, 1914, the last passenger pigeon in captivity died in the Cincinnati Zoo. The species was extinct.

The story of the passenger pigeon is extraordinary, but it isn't all that extraordinary. Many other species have met the same fate. Other animals hunted into oblivion in recent centuries include the quagga (a close relative of the zebra) and the auroch (a relative of the bison). In the last century, the American bison (sometimes incorrectly called the American buffalo) was nearly hunted to extinction. Fortunately, most varieties of this animal managed to recover from over-hunting and are, at least temporarily, out of danger.

Just as the passenger pigeon was brought to extinction because it made a tasty meal, many other animals are threatened by the beauty of their pelts, which are used to make fur coats and other luxury items. In South America, the jaguar, a popular source of fur, is in danger of extinction after intense hunting in the 1960s. The Asian tiger and the snow leopard are also threatened.

The Guadeloupe fur seal was believed to be extinct on two separate occasions. However, it still survives in small numbers on an island off California, where poachers threaten its existence. Other species endangered by fur hunting include the Andean vicuna, the cheetah of Africa, the African black and red colobus monkeys, the leopard, the South American giant otter and several of its smaller relatives, the chinchilla—and far too many other fur-bearing animals to list here.

Whales, the largest and among the most intelligent animals on Earth, have been hunted in great numbers for centuries. Historically, whale carcasses have been used in many ways. The fat was melted down for oil, the meat was processed as food, and even the bones were used. Because whales are so large, even a single animal represented a large income for a shipload of whale hunters.

So it's not surprising that whale hunting has proceeded at a fierce rate since at least the seventeenth century. The earliest European whalers pursued the Atlantic right whale, so called because it was easy to kill, rich with oil and bone, and therefore the "right" whale for the whalers to hunt. More than a century ago, the Atlantic right whale was hunted to commercial extinction—that is, to the point at which there were too few whales left for profitable hunting. Fewer than 300 right whales are thought to exist today in the North Atlantic Ocean.

Over the centuries, the whalers have also hunted the Pacific right whale, the Atlantic sperm whale, and the bowhead whale—pushing each to the verge of extinction. As the large—and therefore highly

Whales have been hunted for centuries. Even a single whale represented a large income for a shipload of whale hunters.

profitable—whales have vanished from the oceans, smaller and smaller whales have been hunted.

As the number of whales has decreased, the technology used to locate and capture them has become more and more sophisticated. In the first half of this century, tens of thousands of whales were killed every year. In recent decades, international treaties have protected many species of whales from exploitation. The nations that form the

International Whaling Commission voted to ban commercial whaling in 1982 so that whale populations could grow. That ban still stands today. But not all nations have honored these treaties, and outlaw whalers continue to hunt whales.

One success story is the California gray whale, which was hunted until the 1920s when only a few thousand individuals were left. In 1937, the International Whaling Commission banned the hunting of gray whales, and in 1970—with an estimated population of just over 12,500—the animal was placed on the endangered species list. Now, the California gray whale population is about 24,000. In June 1994, it was removed from the endangered species list. For the gray whale, at least, whaling has been replaced by a booming whale-watching industry.

The list of profitable reasons for hunting animals is nearly endless. Turtles are hunted for their shells, and other reptiles for their exotic skins, which can be turned into clothing, handbags, or shoes. Rare birds are hunted so that they can be sold as pets. Wild deer, manatees, and game birds are killed for their tasty meat.

On close examination, it might seem that hunters who exterminate a species are working against their own best interests. An industry, such as the whaling industry, that makes its income from a commercially valuable animal species would seem to have a special interest in preventing that animal from becoming extinct. If the animals disappear, so does the hunter's income.

And, in fact, there are international organizations founded by hunters and dedicated to finding ways of perpetuating the existence of hunted species. As you just learned, the International Whaling Commission attempts to prevent overhunting of whales. The International Fur Trade Confederation performs a similar role in the protection of fur-bearing species. These organizations do not attempt to permanently ban all hunting of these species—such a ban would, after all, put an end to the very industries that the organizations are designed to protect. But they do have the authority to regulate which animals can be hunted, and which are subject to hunting quotas.

However, not all hunters see such regulations as being in their self-interest. The sad fact is that sometimes the extermination of a species is profitable, even if it is morally reprehensible. If the whalers exterminated every whale on Earth today and invested the earnings from their carcasses at compound interest, they would almost certainly earn more in the long run from the compound interest than from placing rational limits on whaling to ensure the survival of the whales. And there will always be renegade hunters—poachers—who wish to turn a quick profit for themselves at the expense of other hunters and of the species they destroy.

Of course, some people hunt for the food and fur that they need to survive. Eskimos, for instance, have traditionally hunted whales for food and blubber, and killed seals for clothing. This kind of hunting is much easier to condone than hunting for profit. Such small-scale hunting is also less likely to endanger the future of a species.

Not all hunting of endangered species is done for profit. Some of it is simply for fun—or "sport," as the hunters themselves might prefer to say. Sport hunting at its most excessive can be every bit as destructive as hunting for profit. In past centuries, wealthy hunters have boasted of killing animals in numbers that seem astonishing by modern standards. One nineteenth-century English hunter reportedly killed 500,000 animals in his lifetime. More recently, during a 5-year period in the mid-1970s, nearly all of the 30,000 elephants in Uganda were exterminated in one of the greatest animal massacres of modern times—despite the fact that the elephant was protected by law as an endangered species.

In the Middle East, Arabs have hunted an animal called the oryx for centuries. Legend has it that a person who kills an oryx will receive the animal's courage and strength. In modern times, however, the oryx hunt has consisted of several hunters in a jeep firing machine guns at a fleeing oryx—hardly proof of anyone's courage or skill. As a result of this hunting, the oryx exists only in special reserves where it is protected from machine-gun-wielding "hunters."

Finally, some animals are hunted neither for sport nor for profit, but because they are considered a threat or a nuisance. Wolves have been the frequent victims of this kind of persecution. Farmers and ranchers believe they are a threat to their livestock. Grizzly bears have been hunted for similar reasons, as have cougars and coyotes.

Many *subspecies* of these animals have been driven to extinction. (A subspecies is a variety of animal that can interbreed with other varieties, though it is not physically identical to them.) The gray wolf was hunted almost to extinction in the Western United States. As a result, the ecosystem it belongs to has suffered. Where there was once a balance between predators (the wolves) and prey (elk, coyotes), elk herds and coyote populations will swell in the absence of wolves. Large numbers of elk take their toll on plant species, such as willow and aspen trees, and on beavers, which compete with elks for this food supply. And large numbers of coyotes mean that populations of other small predators like foxes, badgers, and martens, dwindle. These predators all compete with coyotes for the same food supply—rodents.

To save the gray wolf from extinction, and to restore some balance to their ecosystem, sixty-six wolves were captured in Canada and released into Yellowstone National Park and a wilderness area in Idaho in the mid-1990s. Now, there are more than 160 gray wolves in the region. As a result, elk and coyote populations are decreasing. At the same time, plants, small predators, and rodents are thriving.

The gray wolf was hunted almost to extinction in the western United States. In the mid-1990s, sixty-six wolves from Canada were released into Yellowstone National Park and Idaho in an effort to repopulate the region.

Conservation biologists consider the reintroduction a success. In fact, they are now considering releasing grizzly bears into central Idaho and western Montana.

Introduction of Exotic Species

Another way that humans have put pressure on many of the world's plants and animals is by introducing new species into habitats. Ever since people have sailed ships, they have been transporting plants and animals from place to place. In fact, many people aren't even aware of which species are indigenous—native to a particular area— and which are *exotic*—introduced from somewhere else. At one time, sailors would leave pigs and goats on islands, as a food supply for other sailors who might be shipwrecked there at a later date, or so that they would have food if they ever returned. And when Europeans settled in North America, they brought along hundreds of weeds and plants that are now common throughout the United States.

Sometimes these *invasive* species threaten the native species in a particular habitat, and can even drive the natives to extinction. For example, the Australian melaleuca tree, which was introduced into the Florida Everglades, has displaced the native vegetation in some of the drier areas because it is better at competing for the available water.

One of the most well-known invasions of an exotic species in recent times is the introduction of zebra mussels into the Great Lakes of the United States. In 1986, the zebra mussel hitched a ride from Europe to the United States in a ship's ballast water—water a ship takes on before leaving port to make it more stable when it's not carrying any cargo. When the ballast water was released into the St. Clair River—a river that feeds into the Great Lakes system near Detroit—the zebra mussels were released too. They began to reproduce and spread quickly through all the Great Lakes, where they now exist in huge numbers. In some places, there are as many as 30,000 mussels per square yard!

Zebra mussels attach to any hard surface, and have settled in great densities in the water-intake pipes of cities' water supplies and power facilities. Mussel communities can get so thick that they eventually block the pipes, making costly repairs necessary. As great as this problem is, however, the zebra mussels may be responsible for a more serious problem—changing the ecology of the Great Lakes.

Zebra mussels are filter feeders. As lake water passes through their bodies, the mussels eat the *plankton* floating in the water. They filter so much plankton out of the water that little food is left for other plankton-eaters. If these plankton-eaters die out, the Great Lakes' entire food chain is disrupted. This means that the fish that commercial fishers depend on die too. If the zebra mussel population can't be controlled—and the mussels have no natural predators in the Great Lakes—then fish populations in these lakes may decline significantly.

Although introduced species can be harmful wherever they appear, plants and animals that live on islands are especially vulnerable to these invaders. As you learned earlier, island ecology is very fragile. It doesn't take much to disrupt an island ecosystem. Because plants and animals on an island have relatively few predators, they evolve few defenses. So the introduction of even a single predator species into an island environment can be disastrous.

One such disruption was responsible for the extinction of the dodo bird. The dodo existed only on the island of Mauritius, 500

Zebra mussels were accidentally introduced into the Great Lakes in 1986, and they spread quickly through all of the Great Lakes, disrupting the ecosystem.

miles (800 km) west of Madagascar in the Indian Ocean. European explorers discovered the dodo at the end of the sixteenth century. By the end of the seventeenth century, the dodo bird was gone forever.

The dodo was one of the oddest birds of modern times. It was a large, flightless bird that vaguely resembled a turkey. It had a huge head and an odd-shaped bill. Scientists believe it descended from doves that had colonized the island thousands of years earlier.

On Mauritius, the dodo had no natural enemies, so it evolved no natural defenses (or lost the ones it originally had). It couldn't fly, it

The dodo, a large flightless bird that once lived on the island of Mauritius in the Indian Ocean, is now extinct.

moved slowly, and it wasn't very intelligent—so it easily fell prey to the dogs brought to the island by explorers. And, though descriptions of the dodo's tastiness vary somewhat from one account to another, the sailors who came to Mauritius did not hesitate to add the easily captured dodos to their diets. (Capturing a dodo was a simple matter of walking up behind the bird and bashing it on the head with a wooden club.)

The dodo was well adapted to its environment, but it lived in an unusually peaceful ecosystem. When that ecosystem was disrupted by other animals—dogs, pigs, and, most especially, human beings—the dodo was unable to cope. It's no surprise that the large bird became extinct. By 1680, the last dodo was gone. Within another hundred years, the bird was nearly forgotten. It was regarded as a myth invented by imaginative sailors, like mermaids and sea serpents. Then a cache of dodo bones was discovered, proving that the bird really had existed.

Island ecosystems today are no less susceptible to the pressures posed by introduced species. And the island inhabitants most at risk are often birds. Of all the birds that have gone extinct in the past

400 years, about 90 percent of them lived on islands. The islands of New Zealand and Hawaii are home to many threatened bird species. In New Zealand, an estimated 15 percent of the birds are threatened. One of these is the takahe, a large flightless bird native to the Pacific Islands. Takahes eat only fern root and tussock grass. When Europeans brought red deer to the islands in the nineteenth century, the takahes' food supply dwindled as the deer competed for the tussock grass. Weasels posed yet another threat to the birds. Introduced into New Zealand to hunt rats and other rodents, weasels often eat takahe eggs.

Efforts to control the deer and weasel populations in New Zealand have not succeeded, and the takahe population has dwindled. In fact, for the first half of this century, the bird was thought to be extinct. Then a small colony was discovered in the mountains of New Zealand's South Island. A group of the birds was moved to Maud Island, an island without predators. Today, the takahe population is estimated to be about 200.

Another endangered bird native to New Zealand is the kakapo, the biggest species of parrot in the world. Today, the bird is close to extinction—only about fifty survive on two small islands. Threats to the kakapo include introduced possums and deer. These animals compete with the bird for leaves and fruit. In addition, non-native

The kakapo, native to New Zealand, is close to extinction. Only about fifty birds survive on two small islands.

cats and rats eat kakapo eggs and chicks. Humans, too, have hunted the kakapo.

In the Hawaiian Islands, about one-third of the bird species—many found nowhere else in the world—are close to extinction. These include the Kauai akialoa and the Kauai o'o, two species of honeycreeper that may already be extinct, and the Kauai ou, which once lived on the six largest islands but now lives only in the forests on Hawaii and in very small numbers on the island of Kauai. Introduced species are one of the major threats to Hawaii's birds. Polynesian settlers brought rats and pigs to the island. European settlers brought cats, dogs, goats, cattle, and insects. Hawaiian birds are also threatened by avian malaria, an introduced disease, and habitat destruction—most of the islands' forests have been converted to pasture and crop lands.

Pollution

Pollution occurs when something finds its way into an ecosystem that doesn't belong there. By that definition, of course, human beings could be considered a form of pollution when they find their way into environments, such as islands, that they have not previously inhabited. But we'll use the term to refer specifically to chemicals and artificially manufactured materials that find their way into ecosystems and cause destruction.

Ecosystems are remarkably hardy. When an ecosystem is polluted by *organic* materials, it can generally cope with any problems that the pollution might cause. Usually, the organic materials will be broken down into their basic components and deposited in the soil by microscopic organisms. Then the components are absorbed by plants and recycled into the living organisms of the ecosystem.

Few ecosystems, however, are equipped to handle non-living, chemical pollutants. When these materials enter an ecosystem, they cannot be broken down and recycled. If they are poisonous, the threat they present will remain in the ecosystem for a long time. Some of the worst chemical pollutants are the *insecticides*, chemicals developed in the 1940s to kill insect pests. In many cases, these insecticides have done far more damage to ecosystems than the insects they were designed to exterminate.

The first widely used insecticide was dichloro-diphenyl-trichloroethane, better known as DDT. Farmers used DDT to kill insects that destroyed crops before they could be harvested. But it turned out that DDT was killing more than insects. DDT quickly works its way deep into ecosystems—infesting first the plants, then the herbivorous animals, and finally the carnivorous animals.

The most common victims of DDT were fish and birds, but even those species not directly killed by DDT often became endangered anyway. When birds ingested DDT, the chemicals found their way into the shells of the birds' eggs. The chemicals made the eggs so fragile that they cracked open before the chicks were ready to hatch. As a result, several species of birds—including the American bald eagle and the peregrine falcon—were unable to produce offspring. Soon their populations became endangered.

DDT is now banned from use in the United States and Europe. Such controls on the use of DDT and other insecticides have helped both the bald eagle and the peregrine falcon escape extinction. Now that these birds are protected from these deadly chemicals, their populations are recovering. In fact, the peregrine falcon may soon be taken off the endangered species list.

Another form of pollution that is harming animals and their habitats is acid rain. Fuels burned in factories emit a chemical called sulfur. When sulfur reacts with substances in the air, it forms sulfuric acid. This acid is incorporated into rain and snow and falls back to Earth. In lakes, it poisons microscopic organisms, called plankton, as well as fish. On land, acid rain kills trees and other plants as well as some types of animals.

Pollution also threatens marine mammals, such as whales, dolphins, seals, and walruses. In 1988, experts at the world's first meeting on marine mammal science announced that pollution posed a bigger threat to whales than whaling. Pollution compromises the immune systems of marine mammals, making them more vulnerable to bacterial and viral attacks. It also reduces rates of reproduction by preventing conception or causing miscarriage.

Accidental Killings

A popular bumper sticker reads "I BRAKE FOR ANIMALS." Leaving aside the question of whether other drivers actually speed up to run over animals, this sentiment reflects a growing problem for species whose habitats have been invaded by development. The modern world, with its fast and deadly machinery, isn't a safe place for wild animals. When a wild animal wanders out of the wild, even just to cross a highway, it risks its life.

Everyone has been saddened by the sight of a dead animal lying beside the road, struck and killed by an automobile. The sight is sadder still when the victim is a member of an endangered species. One species that is endangered by automobiles is the Key deer, a type of the North American white-tailed deer.

The Key deer, which is less than 3 feet (1 m) tall, is native to the Florida Keys. Most Key deer live on Big Pine Key, an island just 2 miles (3.2 km) wide and 8 miles (12.9 km) long. As visitors to south Florida know, the Keys are dominated by a single highway that cuts through the middle of this slender peninsula. This highway, along with other development, has shrunk the Key deer's habitat, leaving it vulnerable to automobile accidents.

In 1947, there were only fifty Key deer alive. In 1967, it was placed on the endangered species list. A study conducted in the 1970s estimated that there were 200 Key deer on Big Pine Key, and as many as 150 on the other islands. But automobiles continued to take their toll, killing 94 deer in 1995 and 104 in 1996. Today, there are an estimated 300 deer in the Keys. To protect the Key deer and its habitat, speed limits have been reduced, warning signs have been put up, and building and road construction has been limited.

Automobiles aren't the only threat to endangered species in Florida. Motorboats present an increasing problem to wildlife, such as the Florida manatee. Manatees swim near the surface of the rivers and shallow ocean waters in search of plants to feed on. There, they are out of sight of boaters, but not out of reach of propellers. As a result, many manatees are injured or killed by accidental collisions with powerboats. The total population of Florida manatees is about 2,000. In recent years, annual losses have numbered in the hundreds—more than 400 in 1996 alone. These numbers include manatees killed by natural causes as well as accidents.

In this chapter, we've looked at some of the pressures that are driving species to extinction. But do we really need to be concerned?

Sure, species are disappearing at a phenomenal rate, but there are plenty of species on this planet. Out of an estimated 10 million existing species, why should it concern us if a million fall by the wayside? After all, most of the lost species will be insects and plants that nobody ever knew existed. Why cry for them? Why should we worry about species becoming extinct? The next chapter takes a closer look at that question.

Chapter 3

Does Extinction Make a Difference?

Dinosaurs became extinct about 65 million years ago. Does anyone miss them? In the great scheme of things—or in the smaller scheme of individual human lives—does the extinction of the dinosaurs make any real difference? Possibly not. It's fun to hear stories or watch movies about these monstrous reptiles and see their pictures in books and their fossilized bones in museums, but it's probably just as well that dinosaurs can't wander into our backyards. *Brontosaurus* might wreak havoc with the rosebushes, and *Tyrannosaurus rex* might eat the family dog.

Of course, if dinosaurs had never become extinct, mammals may not have evolved beyond a primitive state—and human beings would not exist. So, in a sense, we owe our very existence to the extinction of the dinosaurs.

But for those species that survived extinction—our distant mammalian ancestors, for instance—the great dying must have been a terrible time to be alive. If the extinction was the result of some natural disaster, it must have been a time of great turmoil. Even if the extinction was of a gentler sort, caused by gradual rather than abrupt changes in the environment, the loss of so many species would have created another type of turmoil. Food chains would have fallen apart, forcing surviving species to piece them back together by adapting to new niches. A mass extinction is a traumatic event in the history of a planet, for the winners in the survival sweepstakes as well as for the losers.

The current mass extinction is not a slow, gentle one. With a predicted species loss of more than one species per hour, it may be the most rapid mass extinction in Earth's history. And, while earlier extinctions were the result of natural (if occasionally violent) changes in the environment, this extinction is the result of unnatural changes created by those master inventors of unnatural things—humans. Any way you look at it, this extinction is different from the one that killed off the dinosaurs. And while we may be the direct beneficiaries of the dinosaur's demise, we will not benefit from the present extinction. In fact, as we destroy the environment in which we evolved, we may turn out to be one of its victims. Ultimately, humans may become extinct, too.

Why should we be concerned for endangered species? Perhaps you feel that this question doesn't even need to be asked, that it is obvious that we should use every means at our disposal to save all creatures moving toward extinction. Good for you. Other species have as much right to exist as human beings do, even if their existence does not directly benefit humankind.

But there will always be those who ask, "Why? Why should we take responsibility for the fate of other species, when those species may stand in the way of our plans to develop the planet to meet our needs?" Such a question will inevitably be asked. In this chapter, we'll attempt to answer it.

What Right Do We Have?

Do human beings have any right to endanger the existence of the other species with which we share this planet? And once we have endangered a species, either deliberately or inadvertently, do we have the right to ignore that creature's situation?

If the tables were turned, and the human race was somehow endangered by the actions of intelligent beings from another world, would we expect those beings to help us? Certainly we'd be angry if they didn't—and anxious for revenge! If the black-footed ferret could understand the plight that we have placed it in through the systematic extermination of prairie dogs, and if it could express its feelings on that matter, what would it say? The ferret would have a right to expect us to save it from extinction—and to be very angry if we did not.

But the black-footed ferret cannot express its feelings. Because we are capable of understanding the ferret's perilous situation, it's up to us to act as the animal's advocates. Of all the creatures that have ever lived on Earth, only humans have the ability to foresee extinctions—and to prevent them. Unfortunately, we also have the ability to cause extinctions. Whether we like it or not, we have been given a special responsibility to intervene in the fate of other species, to the extent that such an intervention is in our power.

At least, that's one of the arguments used by people who feel we should try to save endangered species. But it is also possible to argue that our own interests as a species—developing new lands for farming, manufacturing products, and sheltering ourselves—should take precedence over the survival of other species. And this is not an easy argument to counter. The human population is increasing, and as it grows it needs land and other resources to survive.

At some point, it becomes necessary to balance the needs of the human race against the needs of other species. When the interests of an endangered species conflict with the interest of human beings—as they frequently do—whose interests should take precedence?

This is a thorny question, but it might not be as difficult to answer as it sounds. In a very real way, the interests of the endangered species are the interests of humankind, and thus cannot conflict with those interests. The other species of planet Earth are part of the ecosystem in which human beings have evolved, and, in a very real way, we are unable to survive without them. We receive direct benefits from the existence of these species, benefits that we may be evolutionarily incapable of living without.

What are these benefits? Let's look at a few of them.

For Whom the Bell Tolls

On September 10, 1996, two giant pandas on loan from China arrived at the San Diego Zoo's Giant Panda Research Station for a 12-year conservation study. Since the panda exhibit opened, many of the zoo's 3 million yearly visitors visit the pandas, Shi Shi and Bai Yun. Across the country, another 3 million visitors each year flock to the National Zoo in Washington, D.C., every year to see Hsing-Hsing, one of two giant pandas given to the United States as a gift by the People's Republic of China. (The other, Ling-Ling, died in 1992 at age 23).

In most cases, these visitors come to the popular Panda House not because they feel an obligation to support an endangered species—and, even if they did, the support would be purely moral, since there's no admissions charge at the National Zoo—but simply

Three million people each year visit the National Zoo in Washington, D.C. to see the giant panda Hsing-Hsing.

because they want to see the pandas. Pandas are a charming and popular species, engaging to watch and study. Most people would agree that this is a better world because it has pandas in it, and that the world would be somehow diminished if pandas ceased to exist. As it turns out, this may soon be the case. There are now fewer than 1,000 of these critically endangered animals left in the wild, and their habitat—bamboo forests in the mountains of China—is being destroyed to make way for human development.

Some people believe that pandas should be saved from extinction because they are beautiful animals. This is an *aesthetic* argument for protecting endangered species. The world is enriched by a variety of species, and impoverished each time a species dies. We are all poorer for not having passenger pigeons, quaggas, aurochs, and even dodo birds in our environment. Future generations will be poorer still as one species after another vanishes into an evolutionary sinkhole. Every time we allow a species to become extinct, we cheat ourselves. The seventeenth-century poet John Donne put it this way: "[Ask not] for whom the [funeral] bell tolls; it tolls for thee."

The problem with the aesthetic argument is that it tends to support the protection of glamorous species—such as the panda, the tiger, or the elephant—at the expense of the unglamorous endangered species, such as the American burying beetle or the thousands of unnamed plants in the equatorial rain forests. What do we lose if a tiny flower in Brazil that no one has ever seen becomes extinct? Is the world poorer for such a loss?

Quite possibly, the answer is yes. But to explain why, we must look at the other benefits that the human race receives from nonhuman species—benefits that go far beyond the aesthetic.

Direct Benefits

Human beings could not survive on this planet without other species. That's a pretty obvious statement, but sometimes we forget how true it is. Because human beings exist at a pretty high level on the food chain, we need other species to provide food for our dinner tables. Being *omnivores*—creatures that eat meat and vegetables—we eat both plants, which trap the sun's energy in carbohydrates, and animals, which eat the plants that trap the sun's energy.

About 10,000 years ago, human beings recognized the need for maintaining other species as a source of nourishment, and developed agriculture. Agriculture is the deliberate cultivation and domestication of plants and animals to guarantee a perpetual food supply. So far, no domesticated species of either plant or animal has found its way onto the lists of endangered species. Humans learned long ago to protect their self-interests in this area. However, as we shall see later in this chapter, even cultivated sources of food can be threatened if wild, uncultivated sources are allowed to die away.

Food, however, is by no means the only benefit we receive from our fellow inhabitants of planet Earth. The oxygen we breathe is produced by plants. These plants also remove the carbon dioxide that we (and our factories and vehicles) exhale from the atmosphere. If they didn't, we would eventually be poisoned by it.

Plants also protect our landscape from wear and tear. Grass and trees on a hillside protect the hillside from erosion. When natural ground covers are removed, wind and rain can often destroy a landscape.

But these are obvious benefits that we receive from other

species. There are also less obvious benefits that we receive from nature, benefits that the average person may not be aware of until they are taken away by extinction.

From Forest to Medicine Cabinet

Herbal remedies for illness—that is, remedies derived from wild or cultivated plants—may be as old as the human race. Today, we may laugh at people who believe that medicine can be found in places other than a drugstore prescription counter, but such laughter would be misguided. Much of the medicine purchased at the prescription counter comes originally from plants found in the wild. Although modern medicine has performed miracles in its conquest of disease, ancient people knew some things about curing disease that modern scientists are just now discovering.

About one-fourth of all medicines prescribed in the United States are derived from plants. The opium poppy is used to make painkillers such as codeine and morphine.

Ironically, the usefulness of plants in medicine is a side effect of the adaptations these plants have made to survive in their environments. To protect themselves against predators, many plants have developed genes for molecules that are poisonous to animals that eat them; these poisonous molecules cause chemical changes to take place in the animals' bodies. When used in a controlled manner, these chemical changes can be useful. For instance, they can destroy the tumors created by cancer or promote relaxation.

Roughly 25 percent of all medicines prescribed in the United States are derived in some fashion from plants. Without these plants, modern medicine would be severely crippled. The opium poppy supplies such painkillers as codeine and morphine. The foxglove plant is the source of digitalis, a medicine used in the treatment of heart ailments. And the flower buds of queen of the meadow are a source of salicylic acid, the original compound in the inflammation-and-pain reliever, aspirin. (Now aspirin contains a synthetic form of salicylic acid—acetylsalicylic acid—which is more effective and has fewer side effects.)

The Central American country of Belize is proving to be a plentiful source of new plants that may yield useful medicines. In a partnership between the New York Botanical Garden and the National Cancer Institute, researchers in Belize are collecting plant samples for testing at the NCI as potential AIDS and cancer treatments. So far, more than 2,000 samples have been collected. To protect plants that may prove to be the source of valuable medicines in the future, just under 10 square miles (25.9 sq. km) of tropical forest have been set aside by the local government as the world's first reserve for medicinal plants.

The potential of plant-based medicines is great enough that one company, Shaman Pharmaceuticals, was founded in 1989 to develop drugs based entirely on plants from Africa, South America, and Asia.

And in fact, new medical uses for wild plants are being found all the time. The bark of the Pacific yew tree has yielded a compound called Taxol, which fights cancer. Another cancer-fighting compound derived from the bark of the Chinese tree *Camptotheca acuminata* was recently approved by the U.S. Food and Drug Administration as an ovarian cancer treatment. And the leaves of the rosy periwinkle plant of Madagascar produce chemicals called vincristine and vinblastine, which have proven effective in treating several varieties of cancer, including childhood leukemia and Hodgkin's disease. Although the rosy periwinkle has long been used in herbal treatments by Malagasy natives, it is only in recent years that scientists have acknowledged its powers.

The rosy periwinkle plant is one of the estimated 200,000 different species of wildlife in Madagascar. Of those, scientists believe that as many as 150,000 may exist only on the island. But, as you learned in the last chapter, that wildlife is rapidly disappearing. More than 120,000 square miles (310,800 sq. km) of forest—an area about the size of New Mexico—once covered the island. Now, only 20,000 square miles (51,800 sq. km) remain. Scientists estimate that more than 2,400 species of Madagascar's plants are now on the verge of extinction. If the benefits of periwinkle had not been recognized in time, it too might have become extinct.

Animals can also be the source of medically valuable chemicals. Snakes produce deadly venoms that, like the poisonous molecules secreted by plants, have medical importance when used in a controlled fashion. Venom from a deadly snake called the Malayan pit viper pre-

The venom from the Malayan pit viper can be used to save lives.

vents life-threatening clots from forming in human blood. Venom from bee stings can ease the pain of arthritis, and a compound from the sponge *Cryptotethva crypta* is currently on the market as an anti-tumor drug.

Scientists from Abbott Laboratories, a pharmaceutical company, recently announced that they had developed a new painkiller as effective as morphine but without the side effects. The painkiller is modeled after a poison isolated from the skin of a species of Ecuadorean frog.

The curative powers of the rosy periwinkle would not be known today if it weren't for the pharmaceuticals manufacturer Eli Lilly and Company. In the 1950s, the company began a campaign to find just such plants. How many other undiscovered plants—and animals—with medicinal value exist in the rain forests of South America, or the plains of Africa, or the coral reefs off the coast of Australia, or in any of a thousand other little-explored regions of the world? There may be thousands, or even tens of thousands.

Yet there is scarcely time to begin studying the millions of plants unique to these areas before they are destroyed. In Brazil alone, the rain forests are being burned at an alarming rate. A new report released by the Brazilian government shows that recent destruction of the Amazon rain forest, home to the largest number of plant and animal species on Earth, is the worst ever recorded. Between 1990 and 1995, the rate of deforestation nearly tripled. During the 1994–1995 burning season, more than 11,000 square miles (28,500 sq. km) of rain forest—an area larger than the state of Maryland—were destroyed. How does this affect the species living in these forests? As you learned earlier, some studies estimate that in tropical forests between two and five species are lost every hour. And every time a species of plant becomes extinct, its potential medical value is lost forever.

Chemical Factories

The substances produced by plants are valuable for more than just medical purposes. A plant is a chemical factory of sorts, and the human race is always finding new uses for chemicals. Rubber, which has a number of commercial uses, comes from plants. Alcohol is also derived from plants, and can be used as fuel, a fuel additive, an ingredient in beverages, or for medical sterilization.

Plants are also an important source of oil. Of course, the oil that we use in the engines of motor vehicles comes mostly from plants that died many millions of years ago, but the rare meadowfoam wildflower that grows on Earth today contains high-grade industrial oil. Lubricating and cooking oils also come from plants.

As with medicines, it is difficult to predict the contribution plants (and animals) may make to the chemical arsenals of the future. And, if we allow the great variety of plants on Earth today to die off, we'll never know.

Hybrid Vigor

In the first chapter of this book, you saw how species of plants and animals with small breeding populations often suffer from inbreeding depression—a condition caused by the expression of too many recessive genes. The cure for inbreeding depression is the introduction of new genes to the gene pool, which makes it less likely that recessive genes are inherited with identical recessive genes. The introduction of new genes produces *hybrid vigor*, a condition that is the exact opposite of inbreeding depression.

Despite our understanding of genetics, some of the most valuable species on our planet—the plants that we rely on for our daily diet—periodically suffer from inbreeding depression. Considering the vast array of edible plants available in the wild, it's surprising that relatively few are used as food staples for the human race. Rice, wheat, and corn are far and away the most popular. Long ago, when early humans made the transition from hunter to farmer, these and other species came to be cultivated artificially, so that humans could have more control over the plants they needed to survive.

A cultivated species of a plant is called a *cultivar;* a species that has not been deliberately grown is sometimes called a *wild type*. For every cultivar, there is usually a wild type—a relative of the cultivated plant that grows in the wild and that no one has attempted to cultivate.

Cultivated plants commonly suffer from inbreeding depression because they have relatively small gene pools. Thus, some of the most valuable plants on Earth sometimes succumb to genetic weaknesses brought about by an overdose of recessive genes. This is sometimes called *genetic erosion*. Since we rely on these plants for food, we need to prevent genetic erosion.

Prevention lies in the wild-type species. By crossbreeding cultivars with their wild-type relatives, new genes are brought into the gene pool, and hybrid vigor results. The plants are brought back to health.

But what if no wild type of a species exists? What if only the cultivars were left on a planet increasingly plagued by extinctions? The answer is obvious: without the wild type, the cultivated type, too, would eventually become extinct. If enough cultivars become extinct—and it wouldn't take very many—mass famine would result. It is necessary, therefore, that we protect the wild types from extinction.

How do we do that? Wild types can't be cultivated—if they could, they would cease to be wild types, and would ultimately be subject to the same genetic erosion that threatens the cultivars. To keep the wild types in existence, we must preserve their habitats—the forests and grasslands of Earth, the very environments that even now are being destroyed.

The Genetic Library

We can summarize much of what has been said above in two words: genetic library. The millions of species that live on this planet carry within their chromosomes a vast genetic library, a set of irreplaceable recipes for molecules that may have considerable value for the human race. And no two species—or even two members of the same species—carry the same set of recipes. So every time a species becomes extinct, it takes its library of genes with it, and the unique information in that library is gone.

In some cases, that information might have proved useless even if we had had the opportunity to use it. But even if the information were useless now, who knows what genetic information the future might require? New diseases will require new cures; new problems will require new chemical solutions. But the plant that carries the chemical for the cure or the solution may not exist by the time the disease or the problem comes along.

Recognizing the importance of every single species of plant and animal, many scientists are working to store the genetic information from plants and animals whose numbers have dwindled to critically low levels. Other scientists are studying ways of creating animals from scratch using a snippet of that genetic information—the DNA or molecular instructions for making those animals. If their work is successful, critically endangered animals and plants could be cloned. Then, our food supply would not be threatened if the creatures become extinct.

Unfortunately, scientists are having trouble developing successful cloning techniques. As a result, saving endangered species by creating cloned copies in the laboratory is far in the future. For now it is of paramount importance that we protect Earth's vast genetic library by preserving the species themselves.

4

Can We Stop the Extinctions?

The problem behind the twentieth-century mass extinctions is sometimes referred to as the "tragedy of the commons." A commons is a field used for grazing animals, such as cattle or sheep, held in "common" by several herders. No one owns the commons. It is everyone's property.

Think of the oceans on this planet, with their many species of fish and other animals, as a kind of international commons. People around the world hold the open ocean—that is, any ocean territory more than 200 miles (322 km) offshore—in "common." (Within 200 miles [322 km] of the shore, individual nations have authority over the oceans.) Anyone is allowed to catch fish in the open ocean.

Consider the commercial fishers who making a living by catching and selling large quantities of fish. It is in their interest to catch as many fish as possible. The more fish a fisher catches, the more profit he or she makes when those fish are sold.

But there is a finite number of fish in the ocean (though that number is very large). No one fisher is likely to catch so many fish

Commercial fishers, such as these fishermen in Kodiak Island, Alaska, make a living by catching and selling large numbers of fish, a practice that can strain ocean resources.

from the oceans that the fish populations will be threatened, but if too many fish are caught at one time by all the fishers, the oceans will become overfished, and there won't be enough fish for anyone to catch.

When it becomes obvious that the oceans are close to being overfished, will each fisher voluntarily cut down on the number of fish that he or she catches, foregoing individual profit in order to save the oceans' fish for everyone? Not likely. Since no one fisher is entirely responsible for overfishing, each can rationalize that it is someone else's responsibility to save the oceans' fishes. And each fisher knows that if he or she cuts back on the number of fish caught, some other selfish fisher will catch more fish and reap extra profits. As a result, the oceans become overfished and all of the fishers suffer.

This situation—"the tragedy of the commons"—is not just a likely scenario. It's happening right now. Equipped with the latest fishing technology, such as radar and depth finders to locate large schools of fish as well as huge drift nets that stretch across miles of the open sea and catch everything in their paths, fishers can now catch more fish more easily than ever before. In 1950, fishers caught 20 million metric tons of fish in the ocean. By 1990, they were catching more than 80 million metric tons. Many species of fish were becoming overfished. They could no longer reproduce quickly enough to maintain their populations. Today, more than 100 species of ocean fishes are threatened with extinction.

The oceans aren't the only type of "common property " being overused. Earth's rain forests, lakes, and woodlands are also in danger. Collectively, the billions of people living on Earth place a heavy burden on our common property—a burden it can't support. Eventually, these habitats will be gone—and many of Earth's species will be in trouble.

And when those species begin to vanish, humans will suffer, too. Those other species are part of the environment in which we evolved—part of the ecosystem for which we are adapted. Humans can't survive on this planet alone. Like the fishers that deplete the oceans' bounty, we will bring about our own downfall by overstraining Earth's resources. We—human beings—might actually be the ultimate endangered species.

How can we save our common property? Do we appeal to the charity of humankind, asking each individual to forego his or her self-interest—the desire for cheap hamburgers or big game fish, the desire for more land—to benefit the common interest of all? Is this likely to have more effect than asking the fishers not to overfish the oceans?

Maybe it will. Maybe we can convince people that they must stop encroaching on the resources needed by the other species of the planet—or the other species themselves.

And, then again, maybe not. If past experience is any guide, more than just an appeal to common sense may be required. Traditionally, when common sense has failed to stop people from acting in their own self-interest, it has been necessary to pass laws. Fortunately, many laws have already been passed to save endangered species. In the United States, the most important of these laws is the Endangered Species Act.

The Endangered Species Act

The Endangered Species Act was passed in 1973 (and reauthorized by Congress in 1988) to protect species from extinction. Under the act, species can be designated either as endangered—in immediate danger of becoming extinct if not protected—or threatened—not on the verge of becoming extinct, but in danger of becoming endangered.

The Endangered Species Act prohibits the buying, selling, or transporting of endangered or threatened species. The act provides penalties for anyone who sells an endangered species or a product made from the body of an endangered species, or who transports an endangered species product between states or between countries. (Exceptions to the act can be granted, however.) In addition, the act makes it illegal for an endangered species to be "killed, hunted, collected, harassed, harmed, pursued, shot, trapped, wounded, or captured."

The job of designating which species are endangered or threatened, and thus in need of protection, falls to the U.S. Fish and Wildlife Service (FWS), a branch of the U.S. Department of the Interior. The FWS compiles a list of endangered and threatened species. The list is based on current scientific evidence, without consideration of economic factors. That is, whether a plant or animal is considered threatened or endangered depends on how many of that species exist, what the threats to its survival are, and the size and condition of its habitat.

The FWS regularly publishes updated versions of protected species. This list, called the Endangered and Threatened Wildlife and Plants, can be viewed on the World Wide Web. The address for the U.S. Fish and Wildlife Service's Endangered Species Home Page is **http://www.fws.gov/r9endspp/endspp.html.**

As of June 30, 1998, 669 U.S. plant species and 469 U.S. animal species were listed as threatened or endangered. Among the states, Hawaii currently has the most species on the list, followed by California and Florida. Alaska, the state with the lowest density of humans and the fewest disturbed ecosystems, has the least species on the list.

The 1,138 species on the list aren't the only ones in need of protection, however. There is a waiting list of more than 4,000 species that may qualify for protection under the Endangered Species Act. Because the waiting list is so large, and each candidate for protection has to be reviewed by the FWS, Congress ordered a moratorium—a temporary ban—on new additions to the list in 1995. Thirteen months later, in April 1996, the moratorium was lifted and federal funds were released to the FWS so that listing could resume. The California red-legged frog was the first species to be granted protection under the act after the moratorium ended.

The list also designates a *critical habitat* for some species. This is the area the species needs to survive. Under the act, no federal agency may engage in a project that threatens the critical habitat of an endangered species. Unfortunately, this restriction does not apply to private property—and it is estimated that more than 80 percent of endangered species live on private property.

The California red-legged frog was placed on the list of Endangered and Threatened Wildlife and Plants in 1996, ending a 13-month ban on additions to the list.

The ultimate purpose of the Endangered Species Act is to save species from extinction—to halt their decline, boost their numbers, and re-

The bald eagle became endangered because a widely used insecticide damaged the shells of the birds' eggs, causing them to break before the chicks could hatch.

The Key deer was placed on the endangered species list in 1967. Automobiles in the deer's native Florida Keys are the biggest threat to this animal.

Many Florida manatees are killed by accidental collisions with powerboats.

The foxglove plant is the source of digitalis, a medicine used to treat heart ailments.

The flower buds of the queen of the meadow are a source of salicyclic acid, the original compound in aspirin.

The leaves of the rosy periwinkle plant of Madagascar produce chemicals that have been effective in treating several types of cancers.

The bark of the Pacific yew tree has yielded a cancer-fighting drug called Taxol.

The whooping crane was one of the first birds listed as an endangered species. The most successful action taken to protect the whooping crane has been to preserve its habitat.

Wildlife refuges protect endangered species by protecting their habitats. The Necedah Refuge in Wisconsin protects the oak barrens, the habitat of the endangered Karner blue butterfly.

move them from the list. To that end, the FWS is required to draft a recovery plan for those species on the list. A recovery plan identifies the causes for a species' decline and outlines actions to be taken so the threatened species can grow in number and reach the point where it is no longer in danger. As of June 30, 1998, 771 recovery plans had been approved by the FWS. Some recovery plans cover more than one species.

Many states in the United States have laws that complement and enhance the Endangered Species Act. There are also international laws that protect endangered species worldwide.

A Look at CITES

The Convention on International Trade in Endangered Species of Wild Fauna and Flora, usually abbreviated as CITES, is the single most important piece of international legislation ever created for the protection of endangered species. It regulates international trade of endangered species. Devised in 1973 by the International Union for the Conservation of Nature (IUCN), the CITES treaty was ratified in 1975. By the mid-1980s, more than eighty nations had signed the treaty.

The appendices of the treaty lists the endangered species protected by it. Appendix I lists species in which trade is absolutely prohibited, except under very special circumstances. These are the species in immediate danger of extinction. Appendices II and III list species for which special export permits must be acquired before trade is authorized. Like the species protected by the Endangered Species Act, the most current list of animals considered endangered internationally is updated regularly and can be viewed on the World

Wide Web. The address for the CITES Home Page is **http://www.wcmc.org.uk/CITES/english/index.html**.

Unfortunately, there is a loophole in CITES, probably placed there to ensure its ratification by a large number of countries. Any nation may take a "reservation" on a species, thereby exempting itself from the restrictions concerning that species. Japan alone has taken reservations on such endangered and threatened species as the fin whale, the hawksbill turtle, the saltwater crocodile, and others.

The IUCN also publishes the Red Data Books, comprehensive listings of endangered and threatened species around the world. The IUCN classifies species as critically endangered, endangered, or vulnerable. Each entry in the Red Data Books contains valuable data about each endangered species of plant or animal, detailing its habitat, its lifestyle, its degree of endangerment, and the reason for listing the species in a particular threat category. The Red Data Books are the most complete for mammals and birds. The conservation status of every mammal species in the world was assessed for the first time in the 1996 IUCN Red List. Within the next decade, the IUCN hopes to have all known freshwater fishes and higher vertebrates completely assessed. The Red Data Books are less complete in their classification of plants and invertebrates, but this is not too surprising given the huge number of creatures in each group.

Enforcing the Laws

The existence of laws is not always enough to protect endangered plants and animals. To save endangered species, the laws protecting those species must be enforced rigorously, and exceptions made only when they are absolutely unavoidable. Alas, the enforcement of laws such as the Endangered Species Act sometimes leaves something to be desired. A prime example is the case of the snail darter and the Tellico Dam.

For a species not even known to science prior to 1973, the snail darter became famous with remarkable speed. By the late 1970s, this tiny, 3-inch (8-cm) long fish was making headlines in newspapers around the world. What did the snail darter do to deserve such notoriety? It prevented, at least temporarily, the construction of a $120 million dam.

The Tellico Dam Project was initiated in the late 1960s by the Tennessee Valley Authority (TVA). The dam was to be placed on the Little Tennessee River in eastern Tennessee, where it would flood a large valley and create a lake for boating and other recreation. The dam itself would produce electric power for the region.

In 1973, while studying the aquatic life of the Little Tennessee River, a University of Tennessee biologist named David Etnier discovered a previously unknown species of perch, which he called a snail darter. The snail darter was believed to exist in only a small portion of the river that would be flooded by the dam. Thus, the flooding would destroy the snail darter's habitat—and would therefore bring about the extinction of the snail darter.

An environmental group, the Environmental Defense Fund, had already sued the TVA, forcing it to justify the environmental impact the dam was expected to have on the region. Just as the TVA had filed an environmental-impact statement and proceeded with work on the dam, Etnier's claim was brought to their attention. Needless to say, TVA officials were less than thrilled with the notion that construction of the dam should be halted to save a single endangered species of fish.

But Congress had just passed the Endangered Species Act, and it provided the wedge environmentalists needed to save the snail darter. In 1975, the snail darter was declared an endangered species, and the TVA was ordered by the United States Supreme Court to stop construction. Certainly this was a triumph for those who sided with the rights of endangered species.

The TVA, however, fought back. There was considerable sympathy on its side, in the government and elsewhere. In 1978, Congress passed a bill that specifically exempted the Tellico Dam from compliance with the Endangered Species Act. The dam was built, the valley flooded—and the habitat of the snail darter was destroyed.

Before it could become extinct, however, the snail darter was transplanted by environmentalists to a nearby river in the hopes of saving it from extinction. Since then, other populations of snail darters have been discovered in Tennessee, Georgia, and Alabama. In 1984, the snail darter was reclassified from endangered to threatened.

In the case of the snail darter, the letter of the Endangered Species Act was obeyed, while the spirit was violated. No law was broken by the Tellico Dam Project, but a species was deliberately and knowingly endangered, a precedent that should cause concern to anyone worried for the future of endangered species. Whether or not the spirit of laws designed to protect endangered species is enforced may determine the fate of many species in the future.

Last-Minute Rescues

Even with laws to protect endangered organisms, the situation for some species is so perilous that only deliberate rescue efforts will save them—and it is already too late to rescue the majority of species teetering on the brink of extinction. And while there are many concerned conservationists willing to help save endangered species, there is some question as to what methods should be used. Consider the case of the California condor.

The natural habitat of the California condor stretches along the Pacific Coast of North America, from Canada in the north to Mexico in the south. These large birds are *carrion* eaters—that is, they feed on the carcasses of dead animals. They nest in caves or isolated rocky cliffs. California condors have never been common, but in recent decades their numbers have fallen sharply. In the 1940s, there were perhaps 100 condors throughout their range. By the early 1960s, there were only about fifty condors left. Although the California condor was recognized as an endangered species in 1967, by the late 1970s, there were no more than thirty birds left in the wild.

The condors' problem was essentially twofold. Their habitat had vanished as hu-

In 1986, the few California condors that remained in the wild were captured and placed in zoos for captive breeding. Since 1992, nearly thirty birds have been returned to the wild.

mans developed areas near Los Angeles, Santa Barbara, and California's Central Valley. Also, the condors' natural reproduction rate is quite low. They do not begin reproducing until they are at least 6 years old. Some individuals are not mature until they are even older. A mating pair of condors usually produces just 1 egg every 2 years, though sometimes a second egg will be laid if the first comes to harm. Under pressure from the loss of habitat, the birds simply were unable to reproduce quickly enough to replace their own diminishing numbers. Other threats included ranchers who shot and killed the birds because they thought condors might kill their livestock. In the years before the insecticide DDT was controlled, it too had a detrimental effect on the condors' ability to reproduce.

Eventually, it became clear that something had to be done to save the condors—but what? While conservationists agreed on the necessity for action, they had trouble agreeing on what that action should be. Essentially, there were two very different schools of thought. Some people believed that the condors should be saved in the wild, in their own habitat. Others thought the birds should be brought to zoos and other protected habitats, so new generations of condors could be raised there and then released into the wild.

One of the central beliefs of conservation is that an endangered species has not truly been saved unless it continues to exist in the wild. No one argues this point. However, there was considerable argument as to whether generations of condors raised in zoos would be capable of returning to the wild and surviving there as their ancestors did. Further, there was some debate over whether this sort of direct human intervention was even good for the condor at all.

On one side of this argument stood the U.S. Fish and Wildlife Service and the National Audubon Society, proposing a program of *captive breeding* to save the California condor. That is, the wild condors would be captured, taken to zoos, and bred. Then they and their offspring would be released into their natural habitat.

On the other side of the argument were such organizations as the Sierra Club and Friends of the Earth, which advocate a "hands-off" policy. They believed that captive breeding would be more destructive than constructive for the species. The argument intensified in 1980 when a baby condor died in the hands of a Fish and Wildlife biologist. Those who had staunchly opposed captive breeding maintained that the death would have been avoided if the FWS had maintained a hands-off policy.

Soon, however, the issue became moot. In the mid-1980s, wild condors died at a dizzying rate. In 1986, all the remaining birds were captured and placed in zoos for captive breeding. Today, there are captive populations of California condors at the Los Angeles and San Diego Zoos, and the World Center for Birds of Prey in Boise, Idaho.

Fortunately, the birds have bred well in captivity. In 1990, eight condors were born from nine pairs of captive breeding birds. In 1992, the first two California condors born in captivity were released into the wilderness of Los Padres National Forest. Several other birds have been released in California since then, and between 1996 and 1997, thirteen condors were released into the wild in Arizona. In all, almost thirty California condors have been returned to the wild.

Today, there are more than 100 California condors alive, most of them in captivity. The story of the California condor is a conservation success story, though the long-term plight of the bird is still uncertain. Saving the whooping crane from extinction required a similar effort. For some time, the whooping crane has been a symbol of endangered species, probably because it was the first endangered species in North America to receive wide public attention.

By some estimates, the population of these 6-foot (2-m) tall birds fell from about 1,400 in the late 1800s to just over 20 by the year 1941. Why the decline? For the most part, it's a familiar story: the whooper has always been very particular about its habitat, and that habitat disappeared quickly as humans turned it into farmland, buildings, and highways. Furthermore, as it makes the long flight from its wintering grounds in the United States to its nesting grounds in Canada, the bird is a tempting target for hunters.

The whooping crane was one of the first birds listed as an endangered species. Over the years, many agencies have participated in recovery programs for the whooping crane. They sponsored several captive breeding and release efforts, including one that involved placing whooper eggs in the nests of sandhill cranes in the hope that the cranes—close relatives of the endangered whooper—would raise the chicks.

Perhaps the single most important action taken to save the whooping crane involved preserving some of its habitat. In 1937, the wintering grounds of the whooping cranes on the Texas Gulf Coast were made into a national wildlife refuge—the Aransas National Wildlife Refuge. The summer nesting grounds of the whooper were not discovered until the mid-1950s. Fortunately, they turned out to be in the Wood Buffalo National Park in Canada. Protected by law and by the sheltered environment of the wildlife refuges, the whooper struggled back from the edge of extinction. Today there are about 300 whoopers alive, 90 of them in captivity. This is still not a large population, but at least the numbers are headed in the right direction.

From Species to Ecosystem

Similar scenarios have played out again and again in the fight to save species from extinction. But despite individual successes, the overall fight to save endangered species often seems like a losing battle. As the human population continues to grow, it will destroy more and more of the natural habitats of the planet. In fact, by the middle of the twenty-first century, there may be very few habitats left. The rain forests will have fallen, the wetlands will have been paved over. And if that happens, the great diversity of species on our planet will suffer great losses.

Conservation scientists estimate that if only 10 percent of the total land area within each ecosystem on Earth is preserved, then at least half of all *terrestrial*—or land—plants and animals could be vulnerable to extinction in the next 50 years. To prevent a mass extinction, these scientists estimate that at least one-third of the land area within each ecosystem must be protected, especially in the tropics.

So what's being done to save species by saving their habitat? In recent years, those responsible for protecting threatened and endangered species under the Endangered Species Act have begun to shift their focus from individual animals or plants to entire ecosystems. There is a growing awareness that protecting the habitats and ecosystems on which endangered species depend will save a greater variety and number of species—including those that are common now but might eventually be threatened—at a lower cost.

This ecosystem-based approach to wildlife conservation reflects the understanding that as ecosystems are destroyed, the species adapted to them will suffer as well. For example, longleaf pine was

Wetlands across the United States are home to many species of plants and animals. In recent years, many have been destroyed as humans develop the land.

once the dominant vegetation in the southeastern coastal region of the United States. Since the arrival of European settlers, most of that ecosystem has been destroyed, and what remains is home to nearly thirty endangered species.

Just as recovery plans are developed to prevent endangered species from becoming extinct, habitat conservation plans are drafted for critical habitats. So far, more than 100 habitat conservation plans have been approved, most of them for small projects. One ambitious plan—and one that is often held up as a model for future plans—is the San Diego plan.

The portion of southern California near San Diego is one of the most densely populated places in the United States. As a result, development and agriculture have overtaken much of the natural landscape in this area. Today, more than 200 species in the region are classified as threatened or endangered by federal and state agencies. One example is the California gnatcatcher—a small songbird that lives only in the coastal region of southern California. Its habitat revolves around coastal sage scrub, which is being destroyed at a staggering rate.

To save this habitat and the species that live there, conservationists and developers have come up with a plan to set aside more than 170,000 acres (68,800 ha) of undeveloped land out of a 900-square mile (2,330-sq. km) region as a protected area. This plan would be roughly equivalent to preserving one-third of the land in an area one-half the size of Rhode Island. Developers have agreed to give up their rights to this land, so it can become an undisturbed natural habitat for the region's wildlife. In return, the developers will be allowed to build on other open land, even if endangered species occupy that land. Many conservationists hope that this approach to protecting critical habitats will be adopted elsewhere and benefit other endangered species.

Wildlife refuges are another approach to saving species by protecting their habitats. In the United States, the National Wildlife Refuge System sets aside large areas of land and water for wild species. These plots of land may not be plowed under to create farmlands or paved over to build shopping centers. There are more than 500 refuges throughout the United States, and at least one in every state. Nearly 170 threatened or endangered species are found on refuges. For example, the Necedah Refuge in Wisconsin protects the oak barrens, the habitat of the endangered Karner blue butterfly. In all, the refuge system covers more than 92 million acres (37 million ha)—an area not quite as large as Montana.

Internationally, several African nations have taken the lead in the effort to reserve land for the benefit of plant and animal species. Since the turn of the century, large portions of the African landscape have been set aside as wildlife refuges for a wide range of species. But there is a limit to how much territory can be set aside for such purposes. And there are already pressures from many groups to use portions of these refuges for raising food. Allowing agriculture would destroy the refuges' usefulness for protecting endangered species. In time, civilization may encroach on even the wildlife refuges.

The Last Refuge?

Will we soon be asking ourselves where the species of the world will live when their natural habitats are gone? Some people believe that the very last refuge for wild animals and plants will be the zoos of the world. The pressures of the modern world may eventually make it unfeasible for any wildlife to remain in the wild.

This worst-case scenario isn't inevitable, however. There are reasons for optimism. The Endangered Species Act has certainly slowed the rates of extinction, and saved some individual species. Of all the plants and animals that have been placed on the endangered species list, fewer than ten have become extinct. However, fewer than ten have recovered enough to be taken off the list. Recently, the U.S. Department of the Interior announced that twenty-nine plants and animals—including the bald eagle and the peregrine falcon—may soon be removed from protection under the act. If the Endangered Species Act continues to receive support from members of Congress—and the individuals who voted them into office—it is likely that this slow and steady progress will continue.

Of course, many of the organisms on the list continue to decline in the wild. Despite success stories like the California condor and the whooping crane, many endangered species will not be saved by a species-by-species approach. The good news is that this approach isn't the only option. The shift in focus from saving individual species to protecting entire ecosystems—through habitat conservation plans like the San Diego plan—will certainly save many more threatened species, and keep some plants and animals off the list altogether.

Preserving a wide range of habitats will not only safeguard the species that live within these ecosystems: we too will benefit from the preservation of our world's natural areas—and their rich diversity of plants and animals.

In the future, we can work together to save as many species as possible and to make sure there are always natural areas on Earth. The time to act is now, because the great dying has already begun.

aesthetic—based on beauty.

atom—the smallest part of an element that can exist on its own; the building block of everything in the universe.

captive breeding—attempting to save animals from extinction by capturing and mating them, usually in a zoo, aquarium, or botanic garden. Offspring are raised in captivity with the hope that they can eventually be reintroduced into the wild.

carbohydrate—a molecule made of carbon, hydrogen, and oxygen. Sugars, a source of energy for all living cells, are simple carbohydrates.

carnivorous—a meat-eating organism.

carrion—dead, decaying flesh.

cell—the smallest unit of living matter. Many microscopic organisms consist of a single cell. Large organisms, such as humans, are made of trillions of specialized cells functioning together.

chromosome—a long, threadlike structure made of DNA and proteins.

critical habitat—an area that is essential for the conservation of a species.

cultivar—a cultivated species of plant. Individuals of a cultivar are genetically very similar.

cytoplasm—the liquid interior of a cell; the general name used to describe all the components of the cell other than the nucleus.

diversity—the variety of different species in the world or the variety in the genetic composition within a given species.

DNA—deoxyribonucleic acid; the chemical that carries the genetic or hereditary information for almost all organisms.

dominant gene—a gene that is always expressed.

ecological niche—the place of a species within its environment, determined by factors such as what it eats and how it behaves.

ecology—the study of the relationships of organisms to each other and their environments.

ecosystem—a group of plant and animal communities and their environment.

endangered species—plants or animals in immediate danger of becoming extinct if not protected.

environmental pressures—also selective pressures; factors in the environment, such as the presence of predators or a change in climate, that result in some individuals with certain traits surviving and reproducing more than the rest of the population.

erosion—the process by which soil is carried away by wind or water.

evolution—the theory that all species now on Earth gradually developed from other species through a process of gradual change; also the adaptation over time of species to their environment.

exotic—a species introduced into a geographical area where it is not native.

expressed (as in gene)—turned on. A gene is expressed when the protein it codes for is made.

fertile—capable of producing or bearing offspring.

food chain—the passing of energy from one organism to another as each organism on the food chain is eaten by an organism higher on the food chain.

gene—a stretch of DNA that carries the instructions for one particular kind of protein.

gene pool—the total number of genes of all the individuals in a species.

genetic code—the specific sequence of DNA that determines which amino acids are made (see protein).

genetic erosion—too many recessive genes expressing themselves in many individuals of a population. The result is individuals that are more susceptible to environmental pressures.

herbivorous—a plant-eating organism.

hybrid vigor—many new genes being added to the gene pool.

inbreeding depression—also genetic erosion; too many recessive genes expressing themselves in too many individuals; this happens when there are no new genes entering the population.

indigenous—native to a particular area.

insecticide—a chemical used to kill insects.

interbreed—to mate and produce offspring.

invasive—see exotic.

mantle—the layer of Earth between the core and the crust.

mass extinction—extinction is the death of all individuals of a particular species; mass extinction is the death of all individuals of many species.

molecule—a group of atoms that are linked together. For example, a water molecule is made up of two hydrogen atoms linked to one oxygen atom.

mutations—random changes in one or more genes of an organism. Mutations occur naturally and can also be caused by chemicals and radiation.

natural rate of extinction—rate at which individuals in particular species have died off over millions of years of Earth's history. The natural rate of extinction has been about 1 species each year for every 1 million species on Earth.

natural selection—the process by which environmental factors eliminate the members of a population that are not as successful at adapting to and coping with these conditions. Those members that are better at adapting to and coping with environmental challenges are "selected" to survive and reproduce.

omnivore—an organism that eats both animals and plants.

organic—living; all chemical substances that contain carbon.

photosynthesis—the chemical process by which green plants, algae, and cyanobacteria use energy from sunlight to convert carbon dioxide and water into glucose and oxygen. Glucose is a kind of sugar that is the major source of energy for all living cells.

photosynthesizer—also photosynthetic organism; an organism capable of carrying out photosynthesis.

plankton—microscopic organisms that live in water and are at the base of many food chains in aquatic ecosystems.

poaching—hunting animals illegally.

protein—the name for many different molecules with many different functions within a cell; a protein is made of a chain of amino acids that are folded into a specific shape. Genes contain the instructions for making specific proteins.

recessive gene—a gene that is expressed only if no dominant gene is present.

slash-and-burn agriculture—the process of cutting and burning vegetation to clear land for agriculture. This practice is common in tropical regions and is highly damaging to the soil.

speciation—the gradual process by which members of a single species are exposed to different environmental pressures and, as a result, gradually develop into two or more different species.

subspecies—a subdivision of a species.

terrestrial—living on land.

wild type—a species of plant found naturally in the wild.

For Further Information

Books

Alvarez, Walter. *T. Rex and the Crater of Doom*. Princeton, NJ: Princeton University Press, 1997. A look back at the mass extinction 65 million years ago that killed the dinosaurs and many of the species alive then, and the theory that this extinction was caused by an asteroid or comet hitting Earth.

Baillie, Jonathan, and Groombridge, Brian, eds. *1996 IUCN Red List of Threatened Animals*. Gland, Switzerland: World Conservation Union (IUCN), 1996. A list of all animal species known to be threatened with extinction. This edition is the first to assess the conservation status of every mammal species in the world.

Balick, Michael J., and Cox, Paul Alan. *Plants, People, and Culture: The Science of Ethnobotany*. New York: Scientific American Library, 1996. An overview of the history and role of plants in human culture, with chapters on plants used in medicine and the conservation of plants and ecosystems around the world.

Brown, Lester R., Flavin, Christopher, and French, Hillary F., eds. *State of the World 1998*. New York: W.W. Norton & Company, 1998. A report from the Worldwatch Institute on different aspects of the environment, including a chapter on the status of the Earth's biological diversity.

Chadwick, Douglas H., and Sartore, Joel. *The Company We Keep: America's Endangered Species*. Washington, DC: National Geographic Society, 1996. A history of the loss of species in the United States, a foldout chart showing every species listed under the Endangered Species Act with the reason for its decline, and a section of photographs and descriptions of endangered species and habitats.

Dobson, Andrew P. *Conservation and Biodiversity*. New York: Scientific American Library, 1996. A thorough review of the issues faced by conservation biologists as they work to preserve the biodiversity of the planet, including habitat fragmentation, species in captivity, and managing wildlife reserves.

LaRoe, Edward T. et al., eds. *Our Living Resources: A Report to the Nation on the Distribution, Abundance, and Health of U.S. Plants, Animals, and Ecosystems*. Washington, DC: National Biological Service, 1995. The results of a study on the health of the plants, animals, and habitats of the United States done by the National Biological Service, a research organization within the Department of the Interior.

Reaka-Kudla, Marjorie L., Wilson, Don E., and Wilson, Edward O., eds. *Biodiversity II: Understanding and Protecting Our Biological Resources*. Washington, DC: Joseph Henry Press, 1997. A collection of articles by conservation scientists that cover topics such as how much diversity there is in different ecosystems, how humans are threatening biodiversity, and conservation efforts in different ecosystems.

Tongren, Sally. *To Keep Them Alive: Wild Animal Breeding*. New York: Dembner Books, 1991. A look at the role zoos play in saving endangered animals.

Wilson, Edward O., *The Diversity of Life*. Cambridge, MA: The Belknap Press of Harvard University Press, 1992. A leading researcher in the field of conservation and biodiversity describes how diverse life forms evolved on Earth and how humans are destroying that diversity.

Internet Resources

American Museum of Natural History Center for Biodiversity and Conservation

http://research.amnh.org/biodiversity/
Home page of the American Museum of Natural History's Biodiversity Center.

CITES (Convention on International Trade in Endangered Species of Wild Fauna and Flora) Home Page

http://www.wcmc.org.uk/CITES/english/index.html
Information on CITES and species protected under the treaty, CITES news, and CITES-related databases.

Endangered Species Home Page, U.S. Fish and Wildlife Service

http://www.fws.gov/r9endspp/endspp.html

Background on the Endangered Species Act, detailed information and statistics on listed species, and information on species recovery plans.

National Biological Service

http://www.nbs.gov

Home page of the National Biological Service, a research organization that is part of the U.S. Department of the Interior.

The National Zoo

http://www.si.edu/organiza/museums/zoo/nzphome.htm

Home page of the National Zoo in Washington, with links to detailed biographies of a number of endangered and threatened animal species.

New York Botanical Garden

http://www.nybg.org

Home page of the New York Botanical Garden. Follow the links to search their Virtual Garden and connect to the web version of the *Time-Life Plant Encyclopedia.*

Stanford Center for Conservation Biology

http://www-leland.stanford.edu/group/CCB/

Home page of the Stanford University Center for Conservation Biology.

World Conservation Monitoring Centre

http://www.wcmc.org.uk/species/data/

Web version of the 1996 IUCN Red List of Threatened Animals & 1997 IUCN Red List of Threatened Plants, maintained by the World Conservation Monitoring Centre. This database is searchable by a species common name.

World Species List

http://www.envirolink.org/species/

A comprehensive list of plants, animals, and microbes.

Karin Vergoth is the senior producer for *Science Friday*, a science talk show heard on National Public Radio. When she's not bringing the latest science news to listeners around the country, Ms. Vergoth writes about science for magazines such as *Scientific American* and *Psychology Today*. Her first experience writing about science for children was as an editor for the Scholastic magazine *Super Science*. This is her first book. Ms. Vergoth lives in Jersey City, New Jersey.

Noted science writer **Christopher Lampton** has written more than seventy-five books on subjects such as astronomy, computers, genetic engineering, meteorology, and the environment. He has also written several science fiction novels for adults and adventure novels for young adults. Mr. Lampton holds a degree in broadcast communications, and makes his home in Gaithersburg, Maryland.